1

"Stacey and Brooke understand the hearts and needs of moms today. They speak with a voice that's encouraging, authentic and will draw in readers from many different seasons and stages of life that have one thing in common: they need hope. Not only do Stacey and Brooke write beautifully, they also know how to connect effectively with their audience in a variety of ways. Their creativity, partnership and brilliance are sure to continue to expand their reach."

HOLLEY GERTH
Author of You're Already Amazing: Embracing Who You Are, Becoming All God Created You To Be

"Feeling weary? Wonder if you're the only one who's written "a nap" at the top of her Christmas list? You'll appreciate Hope for the Weary Mom: Where God Meets You in Your Mess. As a mom of four kids, including a toddler I found a breath of fresh air within the pages."

TRICIA GOYER
Wife, mom and author of 30 books, including Blue Like Play Dough: The Shape of Motherhood in the Grip of God

"We face the weary times not only through being a mom, but because we are humans experiencing the ups and downs of living life. Hope for the Weary Mom is a must read!! Brooke and Stacey speak right to the heart of the issues we face as moms and women, and point us to the One who is the only answer to our weariness. You will find yourself nodding in agreement through tears and goosebumps!"

RUTH SCHWENK,
The Better Mom

Hope for the Weary Mom

Where God Meets You in Your Mess

Stacey Thacker & Brooke McGlothlin

Copyright Information and Acknowledgements

Cover Design: MASVmedia
Interior Design: Franchesca Cox, Small Bird Studios
Editor: Sandra Peoples, Next Step Editing

Contents

Acknowledgements

Stacey Thacker

Mike: Thank you for your love, support, and believing I am a writer. I could not have done this without your support. Your tireless work on our cover design and website was amazing. Thanks for helping to make my dream come true.

My girls: I am the most blessed mom in the world to have you as daughters. Thanks for cheering for mommy and for giving me time to write each day. You are awesome and I love you very much.

Robin & Angie: Thank you for taking the time to read rough chapters and for encouraging me. I was able to trust you with my heart on the page because you are more like sisters than friends.

Kristin: Thank you for listening to the Lord and for seeing what "Hope" could be. Your love and support mean the world to us.

Sandra: You are a rock star. Thanks for making me sound smarter than I actually am.

Brooke: I can't believe I get to be on this journey with you. I love seeing Jesus shine through your words and ministry. You are a gift to me sweet friend.

Jesus: Thank you for seeing me in my mess and meeting me in the broken place. You loved me too much to leave me there, and called me out into a place of "Hope." May you be glorified through this humble offering and touch every heart who reads it.

Brooke McGlothlin

Writing a book is hard. Homeschooling, managing a multi-author blog, feeding a family, and writing a book all at the same time is even harder. I would never have been able to do this without the support of my family and friends.

Cory: Thank you for just doing. For cleaning, washing, bathing, feeding, teaching, and all of the other things you did so I could have time to write. You're a gift to me.

Boys: You're the reason for this book, but even on the hardest days I'm still so very thankful that I get to be your mama. Thank you for keeping me desperate for Jesus, and for always giving me big, squishy boy hugs when I need them. You're my favorite boys in the world!

Jamie and Meggen: Thank you so much for cheering me on, encouraging me to keep going, and for the way you have served me throughout the last difficult season of my life. I won't forget.

Kristin: You listened to the Lord. Thank you.

Tracey Lane: Thank you for letting me into your heart and for talking so freely about Jarrett. He was a wonderful young man. I'm privileged to have known him.

Stacey: I can't imagine writing this book with anyone else. If I had to be "stuck" with someone, I'm sure glad it was you! I'm so grateful for your words of advice and encouragement, both in this book, and in my life.

Mike, Sandra, and Fran: There's no way this book would have happened without your amazing talents. Thank you.

The Hope for the Weary Mom launch team: No words really cut it. Thank you for your faithful prayers, feedback, and encouragement to get this message out. You are grace to us.

My Jesus: You're enough.

Foreword

You'd think because I've written a few books for parents and, oh, about 300 parenting articles that I'd have this mothering thing down. I've been a mom for a while, so that should help too. But the truth is, at the time I'm writing this, my kids are ages 23, 20, 18 and 2. And I'm weary. WEARY.

When I took 2-year-old Alyssa to get her bangs trimmed the hairstylist asked if she was a surprise blessing. "Yes, exactly. We adopted her and brought her home when she was 6-days old. She's a gift from the Lord."

Alyssa was a surprise. We met her birth mom less than three months before her birth. Do you know what else was a surprise? That even after raising three kids—the feeding and fretting, bathing and battling, caring and correcting—I still don't have this mom thing figured out.

I do have a few more tricks up my sleeve, and I've taken a major chill pill (or maybe it's just softening with age), but parenting is still HARD. There are times I'm trying to bathe a cranky toddler and I wonder, "Why did I sign up for this again?" There are moments when I hear "Mommy!" from the other room and I'd rather pull the covers over my head than get up and make a peanut butter sandwich (which is my daughter's favorite breakfast choice—something I choose not to battle over!)

I get weary of power struggles, of putting my needs last, of trying to remember all the important things like making healthy meals, keeping electrical outlets plugged, and reading Bible Stories in order to plant God's Word in my toddler's heart. And it's not like I've stopped my mothering role with the bigger ones either. They need advice, clean laundry, college essays pre-viewed, but mostly they need a listening ear. They need someone to be outraged about their unrealistic Western Civilizations professor as much as they are. They need someone to ask, "What's wrong" when it's obviously that something is.

Parenting is more work that I ever dreamed of. With kids on both ends of the spectrum I realize this afresh on a daily basis. Thankfully, I have God to turn to. He is my strength, my wisdom and my hope. Thankfully, there are books like *Hope for the Weary Mom* that remind me I'm not alone. They point me in the right direction...but mostly point me back to God.

Feeling frazzled, overwhelmed, unappreciated and downright weary? Well, you've come to the right book. Brooke and Stacey are moms who are walking this road, too, and who are here to stretch their invisible arms through these pages to offer you a hug of understanding . . . and some pretty amazing advice too!

Walking the weary (but joyful) road with you,
Tricia Goyer
Author of *Blue Like Play: The Shape of Motherhood in the Grip of God*, and 32 other books
www.triciagoyer.com

Introduction

If you are reading this, a couple of things may be true of you. First, you are a mom. Second, you are weary, tired, and waving the white flag. You also may have seen the word "hope" and thought, "I could use some of that tossed my way."

Last year, I poured out my heart in a blog post called, "Steve Jobs, Me, and Being Fresh Out of Amazing." Here is what it said:

"So the big news this week is that Steve Jobs has resigned as CEO of Apple. In a letter to the Apple Board and Community he said:

'I have always said if there ever came a day when I could no longer meet my duties and expectations as Apple's CEO, I would be the first to let you know. Unfortunately, that day has come.' (Technocrunch, August 24, 2011)

As I read this I had one thought: what happens when you are a mom and you feel like you are not meeting your duties or the expectations of others and you can't step down? Who do you let know?

Here's the letter I would write if I had somewhere to send it:

Dear Lord, (I figured I should go straight to the top)
I have always said (well lately anyway) that if I could no
longer meet my duties and expectations as a wife, mom,

teacher, and cheerleader to the five others living in this
house, I would let you know. Today, that day has come. I
have. . .
yelled
screamed (is that same thing?)
cried
asked forgiveness
yelled
screamed
cried
and, well you get the picture.

I've pretty much fallen short in every category. I am tired
and not really good for much right now. The trouble is,
Lord, that I need to be amazing and I'm fresh out of
amazing. At least it sure feels that way.

Lord, I'm dry. Empty. Hit the wall. I got nothing.
I just thought I'd let you know. But then again, You already
do.

Psalm 139:1
O Lord, you have examined my heart
and know everything about me.

(So, friend, can you relate to this? It is okay if you can't,
you can just pray for me or send chocolate. I so wish we
could have this chat at Starbucks over coffee).

To my surprise the response from other moms was
significant. Many moms commented that they could relate
to my struggle.

My friend Brooke was one of these moms. She said, "I can so relate to what you're saying here Stacey, because I feel the same way. Right now, I've got nothing to give. Nothing. Nada. I'm tired and don't feel well and honestly, I want a break from everything." I responded to her comment. She later emailed me to continue our discussion. From this conversation, *Hope for the Weary Mom* was born.

Brooke and I realized we were not alone in the weariness. We wanted to find a way to encourage other moms who are like us, sitting at home in their kitchens feeling the same way, so we wrote a few blog posts, established a website, and created a Facebook page and Twitter hashtag (#WearyMom) because we are bloggers and that is what we do.

We took a chance and put the *Hope for the Weary Mom* blog series into a tiny little e-book and offered it for free to the subscribers of two of our blogs, MOD Squad (for mothers of daughters), and The MOB Society (for mothers of boys). We also made it available for Kindle Readers on Amazon for a small fee. In the process we found thousands of other moms who were looking for a little hope, too. We were astounded by the response. God's plans for Hope were so much bigger than we had imagined.

Brooke and I will tell you we don't have this all figured out. This journey is our journey. *Hope for the Weary Mom* has become more than a blog post or the expanded book you are holding in your hand. It is now our passion to encourage every mom who is overwhelmed by the weariness of life with the truth that God sees her, He wants to meet her in the middle of her mess, and offer her true and lasting hope.

Please know we are so glad you are taking this journey of hope with us. We are praying for you. Let's move on with hope.

Brooke McGlothlin
Stacey Thacker
October, 2012

1

Why God Meets Us in Our Mess

I loved watching Charlie Brown when I was growing up. Every holiday we were treated to a visit from this motley crew of kids. They taught us about life and relationships in simple comic strip form. My heart broke for Charlie Brown as he tried hard to kick the football, and ended up falling down more times than we could count. But I couldn't stay sad for long, because Snoopy would show up and make me smile with his shenanigans. How perfect is that?

Do you know which character made me crazy? No, it isn't Lucy in all her bossiness. I have a whole lot of her in me. The character I'm referring to is Pig Pen. Do you remember him and his perpetual cloud of dust? It seemed to me he was comfortable with his mess. In fact, everyone else thought so too. Do you realize no one ever commented about his appearance? Maybe it was because they accepted him as he was. Kids do that. But maybe, it was because they thought, "Why bother?" Or, perhaps they all had messes they were trying to hide too. To point out his meant they had to own up to their own.

Help, I'm Turning Into Pig Pen

Do you ever wonder why God bothers with us? Wouldn't it just be easier if He looked the other way or shoved us in His heavenly junk drawer and saved our sorting out for a rainy day? Or better yet, why doesn't He use someone who has it together far more than we do? There is always someone prettier, skinnier, and more together than me. Surely, that mom is available. She probably even has an app on her phone that keeps her mess in check.

Not me. I think if it is possible I've grown in my messiness over the years. I remember as a kid being mortified if one Barbie shoe was out of place. I only turned in neat papers and I always went above and beyond the call. But lately, I can't get my mess together. Oh, at times I still pretend I have it all together, like Lucy. But I feel more and more like Pig Pen. The mess swirling around me this week looks like a disastrous start to potty training my fourth daughter, too much fast food for my family, and a pending war in my living room between my dishes and laundry if I don't start peace talks soon.

What is worse than all of this is the mess that has taken up residence in my heart. It is big I tell you. I don't like who or what has moved into this space. I can't even imagine why God in all His glory would choose to reside there for more than ten seconds.

Oh but for grace. His great big huge *How Great Thou Art* grace pours over me the moment I feel like I am a lost cause and He reminds me who He is. A brief look into the gospel of Luke tells me:

- He came to a messy world
- He was born in a stable
- His parents—pretty much unmarried
- He chose to walk with messy people
- His best friends—fishermen
- He was known to hang out with tax collectors

- He left His ministry in the hands of uneducated men
- He ate with sinners
- He let a scandalous woman wash His feet
- He rubbed elbows with the rejects of society

And truthfully, He didn't get along too well with all the good and safe people. The "Lucy" types who had it all together didn't really need Him. Time and time again Jesus met people in their mess and offered them hope. And they were never the same.

Hebrews 13:8 says "Jesus Christ is the same yesterday, today and forever." This same Jesus wants to meet us in the middle of our mess, too. He wants to do a work in us and then through us. He isn't going to settle for just cleaning up your circumstances. We know He can do that in a heartbeat and sometimes He does just that. I like how the Message version of the Bible affirms this in Ephesians 3:20-21:

"God can do anything, you know—far more than you could ever imagine or guess or request in your wildest dreams! He does it not by pushing us around but by working within us, his Spirit deeply and gently within us. . . "

Did you catch that? His plan is to do far more than we can imagine. He does it by working within us. He wants to teach us about His character and reveal His heart for us. He wants to whisper in our ears, Hope is here. And in the process He changes more than our mess—He changes us.

"Beautiful, the Mess We Are..."

I love the words to this song:

We pour out our miseries
God just hears a melody
Beautiful, the mess we are
The honest cries of breaking hearts
Are better than a hallelujah
Better Than A Hallelujah, song by Amy Grant
Words and music by Sarah Hart and Chapin Hartford

Can you believe that? When we pour out our miseries, He hears a melody of us needing and desiring what only He can give. Our honest cries and breaking hearts are ripe for Him to do a hallelujah kind of work. I know I need it more than I can express right now. Do you need it too?

Brooke and I want to get one thing straight: we are not experts. We're just weary moms. We are not here to tell you how to organize your home, discipline your kids, or streamline your budgets. These are good and worthy goals that may make your lives easier, but this is not what *Hope* is about.

Our stories are still very much being written. We are two moms who met each other and God in the middle of our messy lives. This book is our honest cry of sorts. He has used mothering to break and mold us. His hands are still working on these lumps of clay. We are grateful He sees the beautiful lovely inside our hearts and calls us His own.

While God is super willing to join us in our messes, He appreciates an invitation as well. If you are ready for God to meet you right where you are and do more than you can imagine, would you join us in the following prayer?

Lord,

Today, I want to honestly admit where I am. I am tired beyond the normal. I am a weary mom who needs a fresh encounter with You.

Please work in my messy heart. Make it a place where you love to reside. Fill it with Your presence and begin working on the inside who you want me to be on the outside. I believe You want to do more than I can possibly imagine. I invite You to start right now.

I know it will not happen overnight. I might take two steps forward and two steps back. Thank you for walking with me Jesus and being patient with me.

Thank you for making me a mom in the first place. My prayer is that my family will be the first to see hope at work in me.

Amen.

Chapter One Study Questions

1. Do you ever feel like the older you get, the less organized you become? What do you think contributes to this phenomenon?

2. What does the mess in your heart look like?

3. How does it make you feel to know God cares more about working on your heart than He does changing your circumstances?

4. Does it help you to know that *Hope for the Weary Mom* was written by two moms in the trenches? Not professionals, not moms on the other side of the journey, but moms in the midst of the mess just like you?

5. When was the last time you honestly admitted to God how weary you truly are? How do you think He would handle the news?

2

When Your Weakness Is All You Can See

Beer and cigarettes.

Yep . . . you read that right. Beer and cigarettes. The phone call went something like this:

"Honey, I need you to come home now. The two-year-old is screaming because he wants to sit on my lap while I'm nursing the baby. The baby is screaming because the two-year-old keeps trying to sit on his head. When the two-year-old tries to sit on the baby's head he can't nurse. Now he won't nurse at all and is screaming his head off. The bulldog has started crying because he wants to be fed (doesn't everybody!!) and I'm going to explode within the next ten minutes if you don't COME HOME AND BRING ME BEER AND CIGARETTES RIGHT NOW!"

He brought me a Coke and dark chocolate.

Super-Sonic Weaknesses

My precious boys were born just 23 months apart. We didn't necessarily plan it that way, but it happened nonetheless. If you've read my other book, *Warrior*

Prayers: Praying the Word for Boys in the Areas They Need It Most, you know I actually prayed and asked God to give us boys! I wanted to raise men who loved the Lord with all of their hearts, who would choose to take a stand for what's right, who would be world-changers. It had occurred to me that there was a shortage of truly godly men in the world, and that as parents, we were losing the battle for the hearts of our sons. So, during a time of self-righteous pride in my own ability as a mother (yes . . . this was BEFORE we had kids) I asked God to give us boys. And He indulged me.

My boys, like any number of other little boys in the world, are infatuated with being super heroes. My life as a mother of boys includes masks, swords, light sabers, and dueling bad guys to the death. There's rarely a day that goes by in the McGlothlin Home for Boys that doesn't involve someone wearing a cape.

I love it. I hope they always want to rescue damsels in distress, bring flowers to their mommy, and fight bad guys. Pretending to rescue those who are weaker than they are makes them feel useful and important. Running around our house with their capes flapping in the wind makes them feel strong. I believe developing these characteristic in young boys sets them up for strength, compassion, and boldness later in life. Super heroes, those found on television, in story books, and (the best ones!) in the Bible give my boys something to pattern their lives after. And that's very, very good.

Yes, I want to raise strong boys. But most of the time, I have to confess, I feel terribly weak.

During that first year of my little guy's life there were many (MANY) nights I didn't think we were going to make it. Both of our boys are "those boys." You know, the ones who are extremely high energy, get into everything, don't take no for an answer, would rather wrestle than breathe, only have one volume (LOUD), and generally leave my husband and me completely breathless at the end of the day. Even as little guys, they fought a lot, and they still bicker more often than not. My inner voice, the one that likes to show me all my ugly, had a field day telling me I would never measure up as a mom.

Sound familiar?

The night I called my husband asking for beer and cigarettes I was in a state of panic. I'm not a beer drinker, and I only smoked a few times in college (sorry Mom and Dad). But as I sat on my front stoop in tears that night, cell phone in hand, toddler in the pack-n-play, and baby in the swing (and the stinking bulldog tied to the chair!), something in me snapped. After months of trying so hard to put on a brave and sure face to my friends and family, I broke down and admitted there was no way I could raise these boys by myself.

Now maybe you're stronger than I am. Maybe you're one of those moms who has it all together. Your children jump to attention at your every command, are polite to strangers, and dance a jig while they do their chores. Maybe you don't scare the neighbors by yelling, "HELP ME JESUS!!!" at the top of your lungs multiple times a day.

But I do. And I bet if you're honest, your life isn't all peaches and cream either. (If it is, you need to be the one writing this book!).

Five years later life is still hard. I don't have anyone tugging on me to nurse or trying to sit on a sibling's head anymore (ok . . . maybe sometimes . . .). We lost our precious bulldog this year to cancer, and now have an energetic lab puppy. But I still have incredibly active, highly distractible, in your face little boys. Sometimes I'm tempted to think I'm all alone in my walk. Those days threaten to overwhelm me, and my complete inability to change their hearts of stone into hearts of flesh makes my weakness blaze until it's all I can see.

The Lie

We moms, we think we're all alone, don't we? We think our problems are worse than everyone else's. We think our children's sinful hearts are more sinful than everyone else's. We think our weak spots have to be hidden, and can't imagine telling the truth about what's happening in our homes.

During those times, we often feel trapped.

My husband works shift-work and only gets to come to church with us twice a month if we're lucky. When our boys were small, I avoided bringing them into the service for communion at the end because I knew I couldn't control them. We missed numerous church picnics, turned down endless play dates, and endured more preschool or Sunday school calls from teachers than I care to remember, all because our boys were (and are) 250% boy. Even people who loved them, and wanted to help them, didn't know how to contain them. Venturing out into public began to feel like setting myself up for failure. And so, to a large extent, I quit.

I wore the burden of it all like a straight jacket . . . bound up by shame and incapable of getting loose by myself.

But Jesus had the key. He had it for me, and He has it for you. It's called embracing our weakness.

Choosing Truth

It was during a phone call with a friend when I finally decided my life was pretty normal. We'd been chatting about church this and that for just a few seconds when she interrupted the conversation to tell the little voice in her home to stop what he was doing. When that same little voice turned a bit nasty and screamed, "NO I WON'T!" to his mama on the phone, a light bulb went off in my heart, and I knew I'd met a kindred spirit . . . or at least another human being who knew what I was going through.

In what was one of the most profound moments of my life, I was inspired to step out from behind the curtains I'd been hiding behind and into the light. One phone call empowered me to connect with other mothers of boys and tell my ugly truth, because I suddenly knew that if I felt alone and desperate in my mothering, there had to be other moms who did too. Soon after that simple phone conversation, the Lord placed a dream in my heart for what would eventually become the MOB Society—an online,

Christian community for mothers of boys. FOR moms of boys, BY moms of boys. A place where boy moms can feel safe, let it all hang out, and find community and help around raising these wild and crazy, beautiful and boisterous, overwhelming but amazing boys.

I chose truth.

I chose to lay down the shame, and open the blinds, letting God shine the light of His Word in my heart. I came clean, and agreed with God that I could no more raise these boys to be godly men by myself than I could walk to the moon.

I stopped listening to the voices that lied to me, and started filling my heart with the voice of truth. It made all the difference.

Boast in Your Weakness

Do you hear the small voice whispering, friends? It's struggling hard to be heard over the condemning voices in your head, but it wants you to hear the truth and embrace it. It's saying, "It's OK to be weak. It's OK to not know what to do or how to do it. It's OK that you don't have the answers, I do."

The voice gets a little louder now as you start to tune in your heart . . .
"It's OK to feel lost. It's OK to need help. It's OK you're not perfect, I was!"

It's shouting at you now, mama!

"It's OK to fail! It's OK to get things wrong! IT'S OK TO BE WEAK, because in your weakness I AM strong."

"It's OK to be weak, because in your weakness I AM strong."

"But he said to me, 'My grace is sufficient for you, for my power is made perfect in weakness.' Therefore I will boast all the more gladly of my weaknesses, so that the power of Christ may rest upon me. For the sake of Christ, then, I am content with weaknesses, insults, hardships, persecutions, and calamities. For when I am weak, then I am strong." (2 Corinthians 12:9-10)

So boast, mom. Boast in the fact that you're not good enough, not strong enough, not smart enough, NOT ENOUGH to be a good mom. And watch what God does. Boast. Be honest about where you are, who you are, and who you're not. Wiggle out of that straight jacket as Jesus turns the key with HIS mighty right hand and let Him be strong for you.

My boys buzz by me, capes flapping, swords raised in defense of the defenseless, and most days I still feel pretty weak. If you walk close to our home, you'll still hear me screaming, "Help me Jesus!!" from time-to-time. But now, instead of letting my weaknesses define me, restrain me, I'm using them to drive my heart to my source of strength. When I feel weak, I find my strength in His words of truth, remembering who I am and Whose I am, and take one more step on the path He's called me to walk.

He's waiting to make His strength perfect in your weakness too, friends. Boast in your weakness, and then be truly strong.

Chapter Two Study Questions

1. Where do you usually turn for relief? Can you relate to the story Brooke shared in this chapter of feeling completely overwhelmed?

2. Have you gotten to the place of total breakdown? What did it look like for you?

3. How does it feel to know you really don't have what it takes to be the kind of mom you want to be?

4. How does it feel to know you have no power to change the hearts of your children?

5. God wants us to boast about our weaknesses so His power can be freed up to work in our lives. Share five ways you aren't enough.

3

When You Don't Measure Up

The dishes in my sink could have their own zip code. There has been a fort in my living room for days. My daughter has pirated all my best decorations to decorate said fort. The baby is wrapped around my leg eating something she may have found on the floor. I'm searching for something under the couch when it hits me, "Where do I start?"

***

I had no idea what I wanted to be when I grew up. It wasn't that I didn't have hopes and dreams.
I suppose I did. Living in a small town, I was happy, content, and safe. My dreams involved being a professional cheerleader or singing on Broadway. At some point, these dreams just seemed a little bit ridiculous, so I focused on getting good grades and attending a good school.

The truth is, I always knew I would be a mom. I loved playing dolls as a girl living on *29 Lincoln Avenue*. In fact, I probably played with dolls much longer than other girls. I remember the last doll I received for Christmas. She wore a cream-colored dress and had blue eyes that blinked shut when I lay her down to sleep. There was a struggle in my heart that year to grow up, and a fight to stay young.

Luckily for me, this also coincided somewhat with my babysitting years. I could now dress and keep real babies who smelled like baby powder and apple juice. In the years that followed, while other more popular girls went on dates, I spent Saturday nights putting other peoples' babies to bed and watching MTV. I dreamed about being a good mom and the home I would one day keep.

Twelve years ago I sat in a wheelchair as a nurse in pink scrubs wheeled me to the curb, amazed by the brand new baby girl in my arms. While my husband pulled around with the car, I remember thinking, *"Do they know I'm leaving here with her? Do they really think I have what it takes to be a good mom?"*

I guess I always knew how to be a good mom. My version was somewhere between Carol Brady and Caroline Ingalls. For the sake of consistency, we should probably call my good mom Carol. Carol woke up every morning with a smile on her face. She whipped up a magnificent healthy breakfast for her growing brood while her whites were soaking in *Clorox* in the washing machine. She sparkled with grace and quite frankly her favorite part of day was when the kids would come downstairs for breakfast. She clearly had a good handle on this mommy thing.

The best part about Carol was she always had time for her kids. She had lots of wisdom- filled conversations while eating homemade chocolate chip cookies after school. Her kids, would say, *"Wow, Mom, you are the best."* She knew it was true.

At night, Carol was tired, but not exhausted. She slept with her make up perfectly in place and a smile on her lips. Life as mom was good. She was good. *And she was enough.*

I see her staring at me with her hands on her hips. She judges me. She makes me feel less than. She reminds me I will never measure up. She sighs a lot, pushing me to keep going when I have nothing left to give. Carol is no longer my role model. She is no longer the mom I believe I can be. She is my phantom. And most days, I just can't seem to get her out of my kitchen or my heart.

***

Lately, Carol has shown up in my house and not in a good way. She is a lot less like the graceful and sparkly Carol I so admired. Instead, she has turned on me. She is critical and judging. Who is Carol really? She is part *me* and part *her*. Carol is everything I wish I was. She is me on my best day and her every other day. The one who shows up at just the right time to make me feel in the depths of my heart that I am not a good mom. *I am not enough and I never will be.*

I have never felt this more than since the birth of my fourth daughter. Yes, I know the fact that I have four girls sounds adorable. I know right now you may be thinking about *Little Women,* Jo, and Marmie and how sweet four girls sounds. Or perhaps you are thinking, *"Wow, I have a daughter and she is much tougher to raise than my son."* Maybe you are, in the kindness of your heart saying a little prayer for me. Bless your heart if you did.

The truth is being a mom to four girls has become a humbling work for me. It is a dig down deep, throw your hands to the heavens, beg for mercy kind of work that can't be pushed aside. Most days I find myself completely obliterated of wisdom, strength, and humor. I collapse in my bed wondering how in the world I am going to do it again *tomorrow*.

I am not so good at it. I stumble and fumble all day long with an audience of four watching. For the first time in my life, I am leaning 120% into the grace God gives me every day. See, in every other occupation I have had, I was able to perform, prefect, and rise above any expectation applied to the position. This has not been the case, and I suspect never will be, in my mothering.

I suppose, too, no other occupation has meant as much to me as this one does. What is on the line is not a promotion or a slap on the back of praise. It is the very hearts of my kids. And it demands a pouring out and pressing on like I have never experienced before.

I put expectations on myself. I feel expectations from others. I crumble under falling short of the expectations of my children. In the middle of it all, I am broken and weary. Recently, I wrote this on my blog:

I've pretty much fallen short in every category. I am tired and not really good for much right now. The trouble is, Lord, I need to be amazing and I'm fresh out of amazing. At least it sure feels that way. Lord, I'm dry. Empty. Hit the wall. I got nothing.

So what do you do when need to be amazing and you are fresh out? For a while, I pretended like everything was normal. I smiled and put on my *M.A.C.* under eye cream and my *Smashbox* lip gloss and I covered up the broken and weary mom with a veil. *I hid behind fine.*

It was far from fine. I had waves of discouragement. In fact I swam in it. I wondered how in the world I was going to make it each day. And if I am being honest, I would go ahead and tell you, I had thoughts that scared me. I told no one.

But the day I wrote that blog post something happened. I said it out loud. I raised my little white flag and I said, *"I am not amazing. I'm fresh out. I am not fine."* I started writing right where I was. It wasn't pretty. In fact it was kind of messy. And in the middle of the mess I did not see critical Carol. I saw a loving God who wanted to meet me in the middle of it all.

I remember a short time after writing the first blog post that would become *Hope for the Weary Mom*, a friend stopped me at church. She said, *"Wow, you were so honest."* I said something like, *"Yeah, I guess I was."* As I walked away, all I could think of was that the veil was finally off. And I was terrified. *What would others think of me?*

One of my favorite books is *The Pursuit of God*, by A.W. Tozer. In it he says:

"Let us remember that when we talk of the rending of the veil we are speaking in a figure, and the thought of it is poetical, almost pleasant, but in actuality, there is nothing pleasant about it. In human experience that veil is made of living spiritual tissue; it is composed of sentient, quivering stuff of which our whole beings consist, and to touch it is to touch us where we feel pain. To tear it away is to injure us, to hurt us and make us bleed. . . it is never fun to die." (Page 44)

To quote my friend Tracie, *"Oh girls, this (removing the veil) is not fun."* It has taken me forty years and four babies to finally get to this place. In particular, the last two years have not been easy. But they have been necessary. See, what I've been learning is that I am not the good mom I always wanted to be. I don't have it all together. I am instead a dependent mom who is learning to live honestly where she is. I am a veil-torn mom who sees that in order to bring me face to face with grace, I had to be brought low and to the end of myself. I am a weary mom, who is reaching out for hope, and holding on with both hands.

***

I close my eyes and finally ask for help. "Jesus, come today. Come here today. In my mess. To my kitchen, but first to my heart. I am in need of your grace." It is funny how, as soon as I call for hope, He comes running. He brings His Word to wrap around my heart . . .

***

See, hope is not a wish or a sprinkle of magical fairy dust. Hope is a person. Hope comes with flesh and blood in Jesus. When I call to Him, He comes quickly. He has no expectations of me. Actually, it is quite the opposite. He says things like:

"Do not fear, for I am with you; Do not anxiously look about you, for I am your God. I will strengthen you, surely I will help you, Surely I will uphold you with My righteous right hand." (Isaiah 41:10, New American Standard)

"Come to me, all of you who are weary and carry heavy burdens, and I will give you rest." (Matthew 11:28, New Living Translation)

He wants to help me. He wants to comfort me. Hope wants to lift my heavy burdens and give me sweet soul-rest. When I am honest about my struggle and I take off the veil, I am in place to receive this comfort. There is nothing between us, and hope reaches straight to my heart.

As I open my eyes, I see the dishes are still close to a national disaster. Nothing has really changed in a physical sense. I get up, and the tears start to flow a bit. He leans in close and whispers it again, "Surely I will help you. Surely."

And He does. "***Friendship is born** at that moment when one person says to another, 'What! You too? I thought I was the only one.'"* C.S. Lewis

***

Another thing happened when I raised my little white flag from the messy depths of my heart. I found out that to my surprise, I was not the only mom who felt this way. Time and time again other moms have said, *"What! You too?"* As much as I wanted to run back into hiding when my friend stopped me at church, I realized that by saying it out loud, I may have sounded a trumpet call for other moms who felt the same way to join me in the journey from weariness to hope. Was it possible, that in telling my story, other moms might see themselves, too?

Author Emily P. Freeman writes, "I believe women need to talk about the ways we hide, the longing to be known, the fear in the knowing. Beyond that, I believe in the life-giving power of story, in the beauty of vulnerability, and in the strength that is found in weakness," (*Grace for the Good Girl*, 14).

My fear has always been tied to the illusion that other moms have it all together and I don't. I have hid for years because I was afraid they would not understand my broken places. As it turns out, I was hiding from women who felt just like me. They were not judging me. They were simply busy hiding in their messy kitchens, probably thinking I was judging them too.

What if instead of hiding alone we clumped? Do you know the game Clump? It is like hide and go seek, except when the person who is "it" finds the person who is "hiding" she joins her. In the end, you are all together in one big "Clump" laughing and doing life together. I like to think of *Hope for The Weary Mom* as just that. We are all hiding in the middle of our own messes.

Wouldn't it be more fun if we were in it together?

Are you weary, friend? Do you feel you don't measure up? Do you know HER? Does she seem to point her finger at you, as well? Nothing keeps us weary like the illusion everyone else has it all together. I'm learning more and more, they don't. But in that moment, when SHE shows up, I know I am easily convinced. What if, in that moment, instead of listening to HER, we cried out to Him? He, who is waiting to strengthen us, and not judge. He is hope. And surely, He will come running. What if after we found our hope in Him, we shared our own life-giving story? It could be a beautiful thing.

I'm game, are you?

Chapter Three Study Questions

1. Do you have areas of your life where you constantly struggle? Maybe your dishes are piled sky high, or your laundry looks like a small mountain. When you look at those visible signs of struggle, what are the first words that pop into your head?

2. Are the words you thought of actually true? If God were telling you how to feel about yourself based on those areas of struggle, would His voice be the same as the one you hear in your mind?

3. How often do you catch yourself comparing your home, job, income, or parenting to someone else?

4. The next section of this book is filled with verses of hope for the weary mom. Next time you're tempted to think you're all alone in your mess, or that everyone else is doing a better job at this parenting gig than you, sit down, close the door, and let the truth of God's Word wash over you.

5. Make a list of some of the verses from the Help for the Weary Mom section at the end of the book that really speak to you. Write them out on index cards and tape them in places where you can see them regularly.

4

When Life Hurts Too Much

There's a box in my room. A recipe box. Blue. Translucent. Etched in cheap silver metal. And it stayed closed for over six months.

When I bought the box my heart was filled with dreams. Overflowing with hope for the future and faith in a God of miracles, I wrote the names of my loved ones on index cards and tucked them away there for safe-keeping. My secret prayers.

The box symbolized a season of new faith in God's Word, God's love, and the power of prayer. Challenged to believe in a God who could and would meet all of my needs according to His riches in Christ Jesus, I hand-selected private prayers for each of the people I love most in this world.

For a month I faithfully prayed for God to help my boys love to read. I joyfully pleaded with Him to provide us with a car (after I wrecked the one we had). I wholeheartedly believed in His ability to bring healing to my loved ones and provide for their needs. And I petitioned Him to breathe life, and health, and peace into the heart of the tiny baby I carried next to my heart who no one really seemed to be excited about but us.

In early September of 2011 we went in to the obstetrician's office for a regular seven-week maternity check-up. I had been feeling much worse with this pregnancy than with either of the two before it. I was drained, and nauseas as we waited to be seen, and remember telling my OB that the morning sickness just felt worse this time. He joked and said it was probably because I had two other small children to take care of. I thought he was probably right.

We made our way to the ultrasound room, prepared to meet our newest addition for the first time. However, it was apparent to me within the first few moments that something was wrong. After several twists of the wand and pushes of the button, the sonographer, a friend of ours, turned to me with tears in her eyes and broke the news: this baby was no longer with us.

On September 20, 2011, our third child slipped from my womb into eternity with God, and I haven't opened my prayer box since.

Closing the Lid

The day we lost our baby, I closed the lid on my dreams and locked away my secret prayers for him inside of a cheap blue recipe box. My closest friends and my precious husband took good care of me, and God continued to provide for my needs, even answering the desire of my heart to miscarry naturally. There were constant signs of

His love and care for us during that season of loss, but a part of my heart closed that day with the box. I put away my dream of having three boys, embraced all of the good God had already given me, and closed the lid.

To those around me, I appeared to be managing the grief well. But the depth of my prayer life took a hit. And a pervasive cynicism crept into my heart, replacing my faith in the God who could move mountains. I was shaken, and no longer sure God would come when I called.

I imagine Mary must have felt a bit like that when Jesus finally came to her after Lazarus's death. Her family had sent word to Jesus four days prior that their brother was sick and needed the Savior's attention. But He hadn't come. By the time Jesus arrived, Lazarus's body had already started to rot, and in Mary's eyes, all hope for his life was gone. This Mary who had once so eagerly embraced Jesus, just maybe found herself feeling abandoned by the Man she once believed could do anything. We read about it in John 11.

"So when Martha heard that Jesus was coming, she went and met him, but Mary remained seated in the house." (John 11:20)

Mary, the one Jesus once praised for sitting at His feet. Mary, the one who neglected serving to share in the Master's teaching. Mary, the one who opened her heart to Jesus so deeply, now sat unmoved by His presence.

Why?

I believe it was because she no longer trusted Him with her heart. *Matthew Henry's Commentary on the Whole Bible* states that Mary "was so overwhelmed with sorrow that she did not care to stir, choosing rather to indulge her sorrow, and to sit poring upon her affliction, and saying, *I do well to mourn*."

I Do Well to Mourn

Mary had lost heart. And while Scripture doesn't give us an inside look at exactly what she felt, it's easy to deduce she felt abandoned, alone, and angry with her Jesus. I felt each of those emotions in the wake of my miscarriage. I still believed God was good, but I closed off the place of radical belief in His desire to be good *to me*. I quit dreaming. Quit hoping. And just sat still, basking in what goodness He had already given, refusing to dream that He might give it again.

My radical faith had gone in mourning.

In the last six years I've lost two favorite uncles, a grandfather, a grandmother to dementia, a favorite aunt, and a child. My husband was a first responder to the Virginia Tech shootings. He worked inside of Norris Hall before it was cleaned up, wondering which classroom held the memory of our friend killed there that day.

I sometimes catch myself wondering what I'll lose next.

I take more tentative steps now, hug slowly, kiss deeply, cherish freely. But I'm not the same person I was four years ago. My heart is constantly waiting for the next sucker-punch of life.

Loss changes everything.

Maybe the lid to my prayer box had been slowly closing all that time, and the miscarriage locked it. After living a fairly uneventful life, losing six people in six years nearly did me in. Add to that the disciplines of daily life, homeschooling two rambunctious boys also born in that season of loss, and dealing with the stress of a husband who works shift-work, and you get an ugly but clear picture of all that lurked beneath the surface of my heart just waiting for whatever it took to put me over the edge.

It was a difficult, but necessary place for me to dwell, and losing so much in such a short span of time forced me to ask the tough questions about life. I looked deeply at the cross, and wondered again, "*If God never answered another prayer for me, if He never met another need, would His gift of Jesus and my salvation be enough?*"

Seasons of Grief

I sat in church one Sunday soon after my miscarriage surrounded by babies. Some were newborns, others yet-to-be-borns, but none of them were mine. I closed my eyes to drown out the sights and realized my hand rested gently on my stomach.

Consciously or unconsciously, women all over the world rest their hands on their tummies as if to speak to, comfort, or reassure the life they carry within. I did it too that day, even though the life inside of me had been gone for two months. As if placing my hand over my stomach could somehow connect me with the life I'd lost, I held it there and whispered, "*I miss you.*"

If someone had handed me a baby I would've lost control. No one did. Instead, I sat on the pew surrounded by friends, but still completely alone, wondering if they had any idea the effect their joy was having on my pain. In fact, the pain had taken me by surprise. I wasn't prepared to feel the loss of my little one so keenly that day. Life had gone on. Grief tended to find me in unexpected places, and I had done my best to move into it, feel it, and keep walking forward.

But let's be honest . . . it's in times like these that all we really want to do is turn around and walk away.

When life hurts too much, we desperately search for a way out, clawing away from the point of pain. Pain, by definition, hurts, makes us uncomfortable, and changes our perspective. And I've found that pain, disappointment, and challenge tend to make me question the God who made me.

"Do You not see me? Do You not love me?"

Why? Why would we choose to follow a God who allows our pain? Why give our hearts to a God who doesn't always answer our desperate prayers the way we think is best? Why serve a God who allows our children to die, our spouses to get sick, our houses to burn, and our kingdoms to fall?

Why are we serving God?

The crowds followed Jesus closely as He healed their sick, made their lame walk, and made life and breath and being enter back into their dead. He had filled their stomachs with bread, met their needs, made their spirits soar as He fulfilled His calling from Isaiah 61 to bind up the broken-hearted and release the captives. But the tone of the conversation changed in John chapter six as Jesus began to reveal the real reason He had come, and question why they were following Him.

"Truly, truly, I say to you, you are seeking me, not because you saw signs, but because you ate your fill of the loaves." (John 6:26)

Why do you seek Him? Why do I? Jesus begins, with these words, to draw the line in the sand. "Why do you love me?" He says. "Why are you following me? Is it because of what I can do for you, how I can meet your needs, or provide what you want? Or do you really love me for who **I AM**?"

"After this many of the disciples turned back and no longer walked with him. So Jesus said to the Twelve, 'Do you want to go away as well?'" (John 6:66-67)

When life hurts too much many walk away . . . turn back from following Jesus and walk with Him no longer. I've felt the pull to walk away. I've questioned God's goodness, felt an icy grip on the edges of my heart as it begins to wonder if He really cares about His children, about me.

But the question that always stops me is this: If I turn away from Jesus, where will I go?

Jesus, who died for me while I was in the midst of sinning. Jesus, who gave His life a ransom for mine. Jesus, who paid the penalty I deserved to pay. His back laid open should have been mine. His face bruised and battered should have been mine. His blood spilled should have been mine. I should have been called a traitor, my integrity questioned. I should have been publicly ridiculed for my sin, my attempts at being God tried before a jury of my peers. I should have died with the weight of my sin upon my shoulders, God's hand of wrath on my head.

He took it all.

"Simon Peter answered him, 'Lord, to whom shall we go? You have the words of eternal life, and we have believed, and have come to know that you are the Holy One of God.'" (John 6:68-69)

There comes a time in the life of every believer when we must choose to turn away or follow Jesus no matter what, because we know He holds the words of eternal life . . . He is the Holy One of God. And that's all that matters.

Why do we seek Him? Is it so He can perform for us, take care of all our needs, bind up our wounds, raise our dead? He is that God. He *sees* us. But if we only follow Him because of what He does, there will come a time when we feel like He doesn't. And then we must choose if we will turn away or follow through the times when life hurts too much because of *who He is*,
the God who bends down to listen (Psalm 116:2), and gives up His all to give us life.

So my healing from life's losses comes down to this: I follow Jesus not because of what He can do for me, but because of what He's already done for me on the cross. I keep my eyes firmly on the cross, and remember this greatest act of love between God and man. I continue to hurt for the losses, but I begin to see a glimmer of hope. A faint blush of warmth fills my heart anew as I remember just how much He loved me.

And it's enough.

Healing

Slowly but surely my heart returned to Jesus. So did Mary's.

"When she [Martha] had said this, she went and called her sister Mary, saying in private, 'The Teacher is here and is calling for you.' And when she heard it, she rose quickly and went to him . . . Now when Mary came to where Jesus was and saw him, she fell at his feet, saying to him, 'Lord, if you had been here, my brother would not have died.'" (John 11:28-32)

Mary mustered enough strength to place her hope in Jesus one more time, and ran to meet Him. And even though her first words seemed to accuse Him of neglect, we can't overlook the fact that she ran to Him at all. Even in the midst of her pain, when she realized He was calling her by name, she went running.

So did I.

I stared at that blue box in my bedroom floor knowing what I had to do, and for the first time in over six months knew I could do it. There, on the top of the pile of my secret prayers, was a card that simply said, "Baby McGlothlin." I felt my heart breathe as I picked it up and turned it over again and again in my trembling hands, and knew Jesus had called me by name.

On a breezy, beautiful day, my family and I drove to a nearby lake. With the glorious water all around us, and the sun making us want to jump in, we took the pieces of our dream and released them. I watched the wind take the bits of paper into the water and finally felt at peace with the Lord.

Restoration

We live in a world where speed is everything and waiting is unthinkable. We want what we want, and we want it yesterday. Healing is no different. The world doesn't stop for us to grieve. There are still bills to pay, laundry to do, homework to finish, meals to cook, children to parent. We have to keep living.

But healing can't be forced. It simply takes time. And as with everything else in life, true healing comes as God leads us toward it, peeling back layer after layer of raw hurt, and breathing new life into our wounds.

Later in John, as Jesus inches closer and closer to His fate on the cross, we find Him once again taking respite in the home of Mary and Martha.

"Six days before the Passover, Jesus therefore came to Bethany, where Lazarus was, whom Jesus had raised from the dead. So they gave a dinner for him there. Martha served, and Lazarus was one of those reclining with him at table. Mary therefore took a pound of expensive ointment made from pure nard, and anointed the feet of Jesus and wiped his feet with her hair. The house was filled with the fragrance of the perfume." (John 12:3)

From withholding her heart, to offering Jesus the very best she had, Mary now humbles herself and expresses her love and gratitude toward Him who could raise the dead. Assured now of His love for her, she shows Jesus just how much she loves Him and wipes his dirty, grimy feet with her own hair.

How precious He was to her, this man who had restored her family, restored her heart. Once closed to Jesus because of what she interpreted as neglect, abandonment, and pain, her heart was now fully open to Him as her King. I like to think that as Mary poured the expensive ointment over Jesus' beautiful but dirty feet, she also poured out all of the hurts and disappointments she had carried in her heart and entrusted them to her Savior once again. She opened the lid of her heart and walked in faith one more time.

Friends, are there areas of your heart that you've closed off to the Lord? Areas that are just too painful, too disappointing, too devastating to open back up? Have you stopped hoping? Stopped praying? Stopped dreaming about what could be because the lid is closed and locked tight on your heart?

I think Jesus might be calling your name sweet one. I think He might be inviting you to take the first step back to Him, and welcoming you to pour out your hurts and disappointments so He can show you who He truly is.

Open the lid.

Chapter Four Study Questions

1. Have you experienced hard times in the past? Share some of the things you've been through lately . . . your hurts, losses, or disappointments.

2. It's easy to say we believe God is good and that He always wants our best, but when the difficult times come, the truth of what we really believe often says something totally different. Have you ever experienced a time when you questioned everything you knew to be true about God? Share that experience.

3. If you ever did decide to turn away from Jesus, where would you go?

4. Imagine life without the truth of the Bible. How would it feel to go through life without the love of God and His Word to guide you?

5. Have you decided that Jesus holds the words of eternal life? What does that mean when life doesn't go the way you want it to go?

5

When You Want to Run and Hide

One thing I know—this weary mom is tired. I am bone-deep tired. It is the kind of tired when everything hurts and I can't remember my last name. I have had enough of tired. Do you feel it too? Can you even remember a day in the last year when you didn't feel it? "Lord, give me one good day at the spa and I'll be a new mom" I have whispered. But is it really enough?

I recently spent an afternoon at a spa called Bonjour. It was my friend's birthday, and her husband treated us to a day filled with pampering. I have never been so relaxed in my life. After our spa time, we had lunch in a grown-up restaurant with real live grown-up conversation. I did not have to stop eating to cut up food or take a small person to the potty. I was beginning to put complete sentences together and think clearly for the first time in weeks. Until. . .

I picked up my three older girls from their Friday enrichment program. While I was at the spa, they were storing up a whole slew of discouragements about their day. As the van door opened, they poured them out simultaneously for me to hear. When we arrived home, the baby added her dissatisfaction at mommy for leaving her all day as well. Within minutes, everyone wanted to know what I was going to cook for dinner. Later, to add insult to injury, I looked down and noticed my freshly manicured hands were dirty and my Sassy Platinum nail polish had chipped. The happy and relaxed feeling melted away and I was left to think how in the world I could get it back.

The First Mama Who Ran

In Genesis 11, we find a mom in the middle of a dark and desperate situation. Her name was Hagar and she was a housemaid to Sarah, the wife of Abraham. Sarah didn't like Hagar much because she happened to expecting Abraham's first born child. It is a long story, something like an episode of Days of Our Lives. The bottom line is that Sarah treated Hagar harshly. Hagar had enough of the abuse, and so she ran until she could not put one foot in front of the other, collapsing in a heap of hurt, tears, and anonymity. Alone in the wilderness she might have wondered what would become of her.

But, God had her precisely where He wanted her—weary and worn she was in a place where she could hear Him speak.

Gently, He spoke her name.

What, you know me?

Firmly, He reminded her of her humble position.

You know the way I take?

Directly, He told her what she was to do.

Is there no other way?

58

But, God did not send her back weary and worn. He had a promise for her to claim as her own.

A promise of life.
A promise of a future.
A promise of mercy.

Thereafter, Hagar used another name to refer to the Lord who had spoken to her. She called Him, " . . . the God who sees me." She also said, "Have I truly seen the One who sees me?" So that well was named Beer-lahai-roi (which means "well of the Living One who sees me"). It can still be found between Kadesh and Bered. (Genesis 16:13-14, NLT)

Here where she never expected—He met her. He had pursued her heart, not because she deserved it, but because that is who He is— in her words *El Roi*, the all seeing God who sees me.

Hiding in Plain Sight

Hagar called God *El Roi* because He saw her. He saw her even though she was trying hard to NOT be seen. I know on the days when I want to run and hide, what I really need is someone to see me. I need someone to see my hurt, to see my struggle and to tell me it is going to be all right.

El Roi has a word for you & I for the days like this. He planted it smack in the middle of a book in the Old Testament. It also happens to be one of my favorite verses.

"For the eyes of the LORD move to and fro throughout the earth that He may strongly support those whose heart is completely His," (2 Chronicles 16:9, NASB)

See, God knows a thing or two about hiding and seeking. He knows all your good hiding places. He sees you because He is looking intently for you. He scans the whole earth looking with one purpose in mind: He longs to strongly support you. The girl who, when it comes down to it, is completely His anyway.

Have you ever played peek-a-boo with a baby? She squeals with delight when you pretend you don't know where she is and you "find her." She has no idea she is hiding in plain sight and you have had your eyes on her the whole time. She thinks in all her baby craftiness she had you fooled. We know the truth. Silly baby, you can't hide from your mama.

When we try to run and hide from our heavenly Father it is the same thing. We may think in all our big girl craftiness we are hiding from Him. But *El Roi*, He is the all seeing God. We can't find a Starbucks out of His sight or a mall He doesn't know about. We really can't go unseen from His all-seeing eyes.

The Best Place to Run and Hide

"Rock of ages, cleft for me, let me hide myself in thee." – Hymn by Augustus Montague Toplady

If hopelessness had a day, it was when they placed the body of Jesus in a tomb and rolled the stone in place. Many of His followers hid that day. Most of them did in fact. Who could blame them? I probably would have been right in the middle of the crew of eleven in the upper room that day.

But Mary Magdalene did not hide. Instead she went to where she knew Jesus could be found. Scripture tells us she and the other women went prepare the body for a proper burial, but I think she went for different reasons. I believe she went to pour out not only oil, but her desperate heart as well. Broken and honest she fell to her knees before the empty tomb. What a picture, right? It is so like us, too. We fall down before Him and think He is nowhere to be found. When really, He is there about to move in a way we could never imagine.

Jesus spoke her name. She knew it was Him. He met her in the middle of her sorrow and she was never the same. That day, Mary became the first grace clinger. She did not want to let Him go. Because she saw with her own eyes that running to Jesus can bring about a miracle.

When we cling to Jesus He does a miracle in our lives too. We need to come to a point where we believe, along with Mary, that hiding anywhere away from Jesus is never going to result in victory in our lives. What happens when we run and hide from the calling He has placed on our lives as moms, is that we end up running and hiding from our source of strength—Jesus.
Jesus said, "Come to me all you who are weary and burdened and I will give you rest." (Matthew 11:28, NIV)

We don't really want a mocha frappe when we are weary. What we really want is rest for our weary souls. We have got to get into the habit of running to Him and not from Him. And honestly, I'm speaking to this mama first.

We Run to a Throne of Grace

What does running to Jesus on our darkest days look like? I'd love to leave you with a strong visual cue for the days when you just have to run somewhere.

In the movie *One Night with the King*, Hollywood tells the story of Esther, a Hebrew orphan girl who ends up Queen of Persia. You may remember Esther from the vacation bible school you attended as a child. She is one of only two books in the Bible that bears the name of a woman. And girls, she is the kind of woman we can look to when learning how to run to and not from God. This movie is in no way completely accurate, but it does a pretty good job of storytelling. My favorite part of the movie is this scene:

She runs for her life, and for the lives of those she loves. Running past the outer courts through the rain, she throws open the large ornate doors with all her might. The inner court is scattered with a few select nobles. She does not see them. Her eyes are downcast, and her heart is set on the one who is seated on the throne. Her presence there is surprising to most. Who told her she could approach with such determination? Does the king know she is there? Confidently she makes her way and stays her course. This is her destiny. She will die either way—unless he shows mercy. But will he? When her eyes meet his, her king, will she see grace sitting on the throne?

This is how we are to approach Jesus, our king, too. We run to Him. Our hearts are set on Him. We approach with staggering confidence. We claim His promise for our weary and overwhelmed hearts. And as our eyes meet His, we see grace is indeed sitting on the throne.

"Let us then approach God's throne of grace with confidence, so that we may receive mercy and find grace to help us in our time of need," (Hebrews 4:16, NIV)

You know what I think? I think Esther's eyes were really fixed on a throne of grace—far beyond the throne of her husband, the king of Persia. I think she was running to her Savior God, who she knew would rescue His people. She was claiming His countless promises. She was counting on grace.

So, when was the last time you ran to the throne of grace with fearless confidence in the One who sits there? Do you need to take grace by the hand and not let go? When was the last time you took Hebrews 4:16 to heart?

Meanwhile Back at the Spa

As wonderful and needed as my day at the spa was, I know I can't live there. My reality as a mom is quite different. My day is spent in active engagement of meeting the needs of my family and loving them well. It is dirty, stressful, and busy. And most days, it is incredibly wearying. The rewards and blessings are not always apparent. So I get run down. I need a break from time to time, and it is welcome. But the benefits of these breaks only go so far. What is the answer for a mom who is daily poured out? How does even the most determined woman of faith not give sway to being overwhelmed? I'm pretty sure I found it here:

"Have you never heard? Have you never understood? The Lord is the everlasting God, the Creator of all the earth. He never grows weak or weary. No one can measure the depths of his understanding." (Isaiah 40:28, NLT).

Jesus understood a life poured out. Jesus knew dirty, busy, and tired. He had twelve men pressing hard upon Him every single day to love them well. He also knew the pressure of the sick and hurting and of the masses. When He grew tired, He knew where to go. He knew His Father would not grow weary. The Bible tells us:

"But Jesus often withdrew to the wilderness for prayer,"(Luke 5:16, NLT).

He prayed. He withdrew to the wilderness. He spoke to His Father. Often. And in doing so, He also left us an example of what we are to do when we find ourselves in the midst of the wearying life as a mom. His promise in Isaiah continues. . .

"He gives power to the weak and strength to the powerless. Even youths will become weak and tired, and young men will fall in exhaustion. But those who trust in the Lord will find new strength. They will soar high on wings like eagles. They will run and not grow weary. They will walk and not faint," (Isaiah 40:29-31, NLT.)

Are you weak? Do you need strength to get up and cook dinner? Are you tired? Moms who put their trust in the

Lord have the promise of new strength and hope that will soar like eagles in their hearts.

Sassy Platinum nail polish can't do that. The only hope we have is a life of complete dependence upon our Father. He sees us with all seeing eyes, understands us completely, wants to meet us in the middle of our messes, and rescue us from hopelessness. He sent us Jesus to show us the way home, with hope.

Chapter Five Study Questions

1. What things do you love to do to relieve stress?

2. How often do you retreat into the comfort of God's Word?

3. Do you see God's Word as providing you with comfort? Why? Why not?

4. Commit to developing a Bible study habit this month. If you need help, we highly recommend the short book, *Savoring Living Water: How to Have an Effective Quiet Time.*

5. If you can only commit a small amount of time spent with God studying His Word, try reading just one Psalm and Proverb a day.

6

When the Gentle Words Won't Come

I haven't had many gentle words lately.

If my mouth really does speak the abundance of my heart (Matthew 12:34), then I'm overflowing with doubt, anger, fear, lack of trust and faith, and a desire to just give up. This is how it's been of late.

I'm empty and have nothing to give. I'm tired, and the only thing I can think about is my utter and complete dependence upon a God I don't always feel is hearing my desperate pleas for help.

And my attitude isn't great either. Can I get an amen?

I went to bed one night wrestling with God. It's happened before, these times when I know I'm in sin. Helpless to change it myself, I call out to the Lord and tell Him, "I'm NOT leaving until you give me peace!" Like Jacob refusing to let go of God until He blessed Him (Genesis 32:24-32), I tossed and turned for hours pleading with God to give me peace. Sleep found me still pleading with the Lord, "Give me peace! Give me peace!"

I'm weary. Battle-scarred. Beaten down from the fight for my sons' hearts. I've promised God I'll never give up on them, never quit, but the temptation to wave the white flag is strong. I've come to the end of myself. My ideas for producing change have all failed to move them even an inch, and I wonder if I really DO do my best parenting when I'm on my knees.

I've screamed, berated, begged, shamed, cried, disciplined, prayed, threatened . . .all in the name of change. And yet . . .

In the stillness of the holy moments right before bed, as I lie next to my oldest and see the man he's becoming, I speak love to him. I tell him mama loves his head and his eyes, his ears and his nose, his neck and his chest, his tummy and his arms, his hands and his fingers, his legs and his knees, his feet and his toes. I love every bit of who he is, and I love the strong, mighty, awesome warrior man of God He is becoming. I love his kind heart and I love his protective nature. I love his desire to learn and I love that God has given him the gift of music . . . all for His glory.

It's a moment of pure divine inspiration.

When God allows two hearts, mama and her baby boy (who's not such a baby anymore), to align and speak the heart's language, he glows under the weight of this love, then pauses, thinks, and says,

"I haven't been so awesome..."

His eyes look down as the shame and godly sorrow I've been begging God for come and visit his little heart.

Why is it that love given freely, washed over someone with reckless abandon, does more to change the heart than begging and pleading? I think it's because of the Son. The same Son who was crushed and beaten . . . who looked into the eyes and hearts of those He had come to save and loved them into repentance.

It's His kindness that leads us to repentance.

Not His wrath. Not His judgment. Not His punishment for sin. Kindness. Love. Mercy. Forgiveness.

That's what our children need from us the most, isn't it? And I'm willing to bet that every single mama reading these words would give her left arm (Ok . . . maybe her right arm . . . but I'm right-handed) to be able to control what comes out of her mouth. We say things like, "I didn't mean it like that," or "I don't know what came over me," but the reality is that we're stressed, deflated, disappointed, and overworked most of the time.

We live through seasons of constant failure.

Sometimes, it's because we're in sin, and sin requires a spiritual cure—confession, forgiveness, repentance. Other times, it's because we're human, and we just need a break.

I don't know about you, but I lose my gentle words far more frequently than I'd like to admit. Usually they get lost somewhere between chronic disobedience and swinging light sabers smacking me in the face by accident. These "on the daily" tasks of motherhood are just things we have to endure, persevere through, and live victoriously over. But when things get really tough, and I find my frustration levels super high, I start looking for a way to rest my soul.

The point of *Hope for the Weary Mom* is to help mamas point their eyes and hearts to Christ. Because as much as we sometimes want God to remove us from our messes, more often He just gets in it with us—lifting our heads, giving us strength, helping us put one foot in front of the other as we slosh our way through it (see the intro!).

But it is nice to have some practical tools in our back pockets for those days that just seem out of control. What's a weary mom to do to find some rest in the midst of the crazy?

Here are a few free (or really cheap) things that bring this weary mom rest.

1. Prayer.

It might seem cheesy, but connecting my heart with God on a regular basis helps me maintain His eternal perspective when it's all too easy for me to lose mine. The only thing this'll cost you is time.

2. Reading the story of King David (again).

The story of David never ceases to remind me that no matter how many times I mess up, I serve a God who redeems. Moms, we're living in His story, not the other way around, and we need to remember it. Find it starting in 1 Samuel 16.

3. Allow your children to experience the beauty of quiet time.

Even the older ones. Reading for an hour each day might just save your sanity, and providing your kiddos with enough quality books to keep their attention is as easy as a library visit. We bought our boys iPod Nanos for their birthdays this year because they're too young to read on their own. But they LOVE audio books. Nano is great because there are no games and no way to access the internet.

4. Turn on the music.

Seems simple, doesn't it? But it's amazing how often I forget that choosing to praise God through song (whether I feel like it or not) has the power to totally transform my heart. Need a soft, tender, worshipful recommendation? We HIGHLY recommend the solo piano music of David Nevue. But don't forget you don't have to listen to music that talks about Jesus all the time to feel better. I grew up in the country, and when I want some feel-good music to lighten my mood, I often choose some of the down-home, family-loving, corn-growing country music I was raised on. Use discernment when it comes to song choice (measure it by Philippians 4:8), but give yourself permission to have fun.

5. Take a walk . . . alone.

My husband is wonderful about letting me have this time when our schedule allows it. I like to walk during golden hour (morning or evening) and strap on my big girl camera for the ride. It's a double blessing for me because exercising cleanses my mind, and making beautiful photos . . .well . . . that's the next tip.

6. Make beautiful photos.

Take your camera with you everywhere you go. Be one of those crazy light chasers who isn't afraid to pull over for a great shot. Make your children bend down to look at the beauty of God's creation and document it as you go. It's simply astounding how capturing the beautiful moments of my life brings me joy and peace. No big girl camera? No worries. Just whip out your phone or point and shoot camera and go on a hunt for beauty. You won't be disappointed. Beauty waits for the eye of its beholder. We have to look for it to really see it.

7. Create a mini spa at home.

You can get a candle and lovely-smelling bubble bath at Walmart for less than $5. Cut up some cucumbers and put them on your eyes, close the door, slip into some warm water, and breathe.

8. Invest in things that make you say "ahhhhhh."

For me, it's a cup of smooth, strong Joe after we get the boys to bed. Maybe you love tea, or maybe a glass of milk at night makes you slow down and close your eyes in bliss. Whatever it is that puts a smile on your face, indulge in it . . . as much as you can (and as much as is healthy). Do little things to bring joy to your heart.

9. Light a candle.

Even when it's not next to a steamy hot bubble bath, there's just something about a flickering candle and a lovely aroma that brings me joy. Pick your favorite scent and savor it when life gets too tough. My husband and I look forward to fall each year because we get to breathe in our favorite scents. An environment that smells good can literally change your day.

10. Get up crazy early to read the Word.

Spend 30 minutes hiding God's Word in your heart at 3:30 in the morning. Then go back to bed and wake up when your kids get up. There's no other thing you can do that will bring you as much peace as getting in to the Bible. Not even eating healthy . . . and really . . . that should be on this list somewhere (but I am who I am, yeah?). Even if you don't like the crazy early idea (I affectionately refer to it as "obscene-thirty"), still make time for your relationship with God. Somehow.

11. Make a list of things you love about your children.

Write them on individual sticky notes, and place them all over your house. If your children are older, they'll be bathed in love and affection, and filled with confidence by your words of affirmation. If they're younger and can't read, be sure to explain what the notes are and what they say. Watch your children bloom as your tenderness—kindness—woos them to your heart.

Just like God's kindness did for you.

Bonus: Need a practical way to tuck the truths of this book in your heart? Download a free copy of *Hope for Your Heart,* a printable we created with weary moms in mind, at our resource page www.hopeforthe700wearymom.com/book-resources.

Chapter Six Study Questions

1. Be honest about the state of your heart and life right now. Are you disappointed with the hand you've been dealt? Share some of your story.

2. What does being weary look like in your home? Describe the physical as well as emotional toll weariness takes on you.

3. Where do you turn first for comfort and relief?

4. Think back to the time when you accepted Christ. What drew you to Him?

5. Make an actual list of the things you love about your children. Commit to sharing at least one of these things with them every day.

7

When You Come to the End of Yourself

My grandpa turned 90 on 11/11/11. I can still see the old black and white picture my grandma used to keep of him in his Army uniform. Handsome and determined, he carved out a good living for his family in a small town.

His mama, my great grandma, was a weary mom. He was her baby. And when she was so weary she couldn't take it anymore, she left him with his oldest sister. My great grandfather was an alcoholic, and the truth be told, my great grandma had had enough of life as mom, and babies, and figuring out how to put one foot in front of the other. So she left. I think of my granddaddy as a little boy holding on to his sister's hand. I wonder if he ever asked where his mama went? Could he understand the kind of weary that finds it easier to leave?

Her blood runs through my heart. I understand. I'm a weary mom too. But how do I learn from the legacy of leaving? How do I fight with all I am to love deeper, longer, and harder than she could? When you or I need a fresh filling up of our poured out lives, what can we do? I believe the answer is that we need to worship, because anything less than the very presence of the Lord will never suffice.

"Worship rolls out the red carpet for the presence of the Lord." - Priscilla Shirer

My heart knew it needed to worship. God as usual, was one step ahead of me and orchestrated a moment of worship for my heart last fall during a church service. I love when He does that. It was as though He made an appointment with only me at the altar. See I came that particular morning a dried up well. I was a broken mess of a mom. My husband had been out of town for about a week, and I was at the end of myself. We sang all Sunday long until I could not sing anymore. I found my heart being stirred and so I went to spend time bowed low with the One who had whispered, "Come." I confess, I don't go to the altar often. But I knew where He wanted to meet me that morning. And meet me He did.

As soon as my knees hit the carpet, the words began to pour out. Admitting my sins, one by one they rolled out. I can't do this. I can't do this. . . I am such a disappointment as a mom. Oh, how I've yelled. I'm so sorry, Lord. I began to cry ugly. He was gentle and loving in His quiet response to me.

I sat at the altar, a heap of tears flowing down, knowing that in His grace He covers everything. Every. Single. Thing. And not once does He disappoint or condemn.

Isaiah 61:3 reminds us that His desire is to "give me a garment of praise instead of a faint spirit." This is exactly what He did for me that morning. I left with my weariness laid down and a hope filled heart for the first time in weeks.

We were made for worship and nothing makes the weariness flee more than laying down our smallness and basking in the glory of One called holy and true. Do you know the hymn "Turn Your Eyes upon Jesus"? It has always been my favorite because of this line:

Turn your eyes upon Jesus, look full in His wonderful face. And the things of earth will grow strangely dim, in the light of His glory and grace.

It is sometimes easier for me to look full in His wonderful face at church while my kids are busy at Sunday school and my pastor has delivered the Word of God on a platter for my heart. Moments like I described above don't happen every Sunday. Most of the time I feel pretty okay while I'm sitting in the pew. I don't know about you, but I need His glory and grace more on plain old Tuesday when I'm crying in my coffee cup wondering how I'm going to make it through the day. So how do we roll out the red carpet for the presence of the Lord Monday through Saturday? How do we worship in the small places of our lives and make the most difference in how we live them?

Gratitude Leads to Worship

If worship rolls out the red carpet for the presence of the Lord, then gratitude is the thread the carpet is made from. I learned this lesson over the past year as I accepted the dare to find one thousands gifts to be grateful for in 2012. The Joy Dare, given by Ann Voskamp, is the habit of counting only three gifts each day. She said recently on her blog, A Holy Experience:

"It's habits that can imprison you and it's habits that can free you and when thanks to God becomes a habit, so joy in God becomes your life," (January 5, 2012).

Weariness for me is a habit of my heart. I get bogged down by the things of life because—let's face it—life is hard. I don't want to be imprisoned by my weariness habit anymore. My thanksgiving, my daily counting joy-filled gifts unlocks the prison and sets me free. Author Sarah Young says in her book *Jesus Calling*:

"Each day is a precious gift from My Father. How ridiculous to grasp for future gifts when today's is set before you! Receive today's gift gratefully, unwrapping it tenderly and delving into its depths. As you savor this gift, you find Me," (pg 36).

As I am purposefully grateful for daily gifts all around me, joy fills my heart and I find Jesus right there at the kitchen table, while taking a walk with my girls, or tucking them into bed. When I find Him, my heart can't help but worship.

Some days, the joy gifts bubble up. And some days, it seems, pour gloom. Take last week for instance. It rained. Like a lot. We were stuck indoors for days and my kids were crazy. I found myself dreadfully unmotivated and wondering how in the world I was ever going to get moving. And then I read this verse. . .

"Splendor and majesty are before him, strength and joy are in his dwelling place,"
(1 Chronicles 16:27, NIV).

I wonder how long it will take until this truth truly sinks down deep in my heart? I am a dreadfully slow learner. Here I am counting gifts, looking for reasons for joy and really the only one I need is here. The joy dwelling place is found in the Lord. Do I want joy to overflow? Do I need strength for unmotivated days? Yes. And Yes. Do you?

It isn't really all that difficult. Let's go to the joy dwelling place and take a good long look at His splendor and majesty. I'm guessing when we do, even rainy days and Mondays won't get us down. We'll count them, too. And the joy will spread.

Let Your Heart Sing

One of my all time favorite books is *Hinds Feet in High Places* by Hannah Hurnard. The main character is a girl named Much-Afraid (go ahead and insert my name here). In this beautiful allegory, Much-Afraid is invited to go to the high places by the Good Shepherd. She must take a long journey to get there, and along the way she encounters many difficulties. She climbs mountains, walks in the desert, and survives storms. The chapter in the book that has always spoken most clearly to my heart is entitled, "Into the Mist." Here's an excerpt:

"Now there was nothing but tameness, just a trudge, trudge forward, day after day, able to see nothing except for white clinging mist which hung about the mountains without a gleam of sunshine breaking through" (pg 90).

Much-Afraid was overwhelmed by her situation. She grew weary by the moment and began to listen to the voices of Resentment, Bitterness, and Self-pity. This "made her very disagreeable and difficult to deal with." (pg 90). She stumbled about and limped along directionless. She was completely miserable and on the verge of giving up all together.

Sound familiar?

Are you trudging along overwhelmed by the daily exhausting, never-ending task of mothering? Do you wonder if you are on the right path and if the way you are taking is in fact getting you anywhere? Have Resentment, Bitterness, and Self-Pity shown up in your home and made themselves permanent house guests? Have you come to the very end of yourself?

If you just closed your eyes and raised your hand in agreement, sister I am right there with you. See, this weary mom thing is not something I have lived, learned, and moved on from. It is what I'm living and writing my way through right now. As I put words on paper to hopefully encourage your heart, I'm speaking to mine too. I have not arrived. I am a work in progress standing side by side with you.

So what can we do with all this trudging around in the mist of weariness? What did Much-Afraid do?

"At last, one afternoon, when the only word which at all described her progress is to say that she was slithering along the path, all muddy and wet and bedraggled from constant slips, she decided to sing," (pg 90).

The most amazing thing happened as she sang—she cheered a bit. The voices of Resentment, Bitterness, and Self-pity faded away, and to her great surprise she saw the Good Shepherd coming toward her.

"It is just impossible to describe in words the joy of Much-Afraid when she saw him really coming toward them on that dreary mountain path, where everything had been swallowed up for so long in the horrible mist and everything she touched had been so cold and clammy. Now with his coming the mist was rapidly clearing away and a real gleam of sunshine—the first they had seen for days—broke through at last," (pg 91).

Oh how I love this sweet book. I see myself in the pages each time I read the words. And you want to hear something funny? I absolutely love to sing. But some days, when I just want to give up, I forget that. I forget the song God Himself has written on my heart. Instead I listen to voices all around me that tell me to eat a mini pint of java chip ice cream and call my mom to complain. I think I'm alone in my journey and I forget my Good Shepherd is right there with me the whole time. It seems so simple, but girls we have got to find a song to sing on the most weary-filled days. But where can we find a song?

I Need Thee Every Hour

I grew up in a tiny Baptist church in a small town in southern Indiana. We had old fashion hymn sings every

Sunday night. The pastor would say, "What song do you want to sing?" And one by one people would holler out their favorites. Luckily, Lois sat at the piano and she knew them all by heart. We'd all sing together the first and last verse and at the end, someone would say, "Amen."

These days, in the contemporary worship service I attend we don't sing a lot of hymns. But that doesn't stop the Lord from dropping them into my heart from time to time with a sweet memory. One day a while back, I was getting my girls ready for bed and the words to *I Need Thee Every Hour* came to mind:

I need Thee.
Oh I need Thee.
Every hour I need Thee.
Oh bless me now my Savior,
I come to thee.

And just like that the words stuck. I sang it all week. It became a prayer of sorts as I went about my days. Like Much-Afraid, my heart was lifted and my eyes turned toward Jesus.

Now this is the point where I get to tell you that sometimes Jesus likes to show off for me. He likes to add an exclamation point in my life when I least expect it. Does He do that for you, too? I'm sure He does. So the story continues with me once again sitting in church the following Sunday. Remember me saying we don't sing a lot of hymns these days? Remember me telling you that I grew up on them? Well, guess what hymn our worship leader began to play? I am not even kidding you when I say he started playing *I Need Thee Every Hour*. I almost fell over right there on the spot. The Good Shepherd slipped into the pew beside me, put His arm around me and said, "Sweet girl, you must have a song to sing." I cried tears of joy. My heart worshipped.

This whole event left me breathless for Jesus in a way I had not been in quite sometime. I became curious about this hymn so I looked it up online. I found out it was written by a girl like me. A housewife in Brooklyn named Annie Hawks wrote it in her kitchen in June 1872. Do you think maybe she was feeling a little weary and worn as well? Was this the song she was singing in order to better fix her eyes on Jesus? I think maybe that might be the case.

See the thing about worship is that it acknowledges in the very deepest part of our souls that we need Him. We can't take this journey on our own. We need the very presence of the Lord to strengthen and guide us. We need Him every hour. Here is where we find hope.

Where are you today? Do you need to spend some time today bowed low with the Grace Giver? Do you need to lay down the weariness you have been wearing? He wants to meet you. He may have an appointment with you at the altar or maybe He just wants you to sing a song in the kitchen just for Him. Either way, He wants to whisper into your heart that He loves you and will never let you go. I promise, when you come to the end of yourself and you choose to worship anyway, your weary heart will sing once more, with hope.

Chapter Seven Study Questions

1. Have you ever just wanted to walk away?

2. Stacey and Brooke both have family members who walked away when the weariness became too much. What has kept you from leaving in the past?

3. Some people think the only place where you can find an altar is at church. But that's not true! God, because of Jesus, is available anywhere, anytime to His people! If there's something you need to confess, something that's weighing on your heart or keeping you from experiencing joy in your life, quiet yourself where you are and talk to God about it.

4. Share some interesting places you've knelt at the altar of God in the past. (Example: In the woods, on the toilet, in bed at night, in front of the Christmas tree, etc.)

5. Think of a special place in your home that might double as an altar. What could you do to make it a special place for you to talk to God?

8

When You Just Want to Give Up

A mother's heart labors over her children. Pulling, tugging, coaxing, dragging, pushing, begging . . . all in the name of love.

Those of us who really look see our children not just as they are, but as they can be, might be one day. Something beautiful, something great. A work of art. Lives that were once knit together in our wombs or hearts, fearfully and wonderfully made, beautifully fashioned after the image of God. We look with longing and wonder what the Master Weaver might create.

It's sweaty work—manual labor of the most intense kind because it requires more than just body. Mothering demands body, soul, mind, and heart. And when the work doesn't pay off . . . when the pulling and tugging and coaxing and dragging and pushing and begging and praying don't seem to change anything, we can be left empty, exhausted, worn down. Wanting to just give up. Weary.

In a season of searching for the gentle words and not finding them, two months of morning sickness, two weeks of vertigo, and a miscarriage that shook my world, I found myself helpless and hopeless. Helpless because it had truly dawned on me that I had no power to change the hearts of my children. Hopeless because God wasn't answering my prayers to change them. I felt like giving up. I didn't want to pray anymore. Not because I stopped loving God, but because I wondered if my prayers truly meant anything to Him. I was sweaty, empty, exhausted, and worn down.

So I quit. Just for a season I stopped the voice in my heart that tells me the way to go. As He tried to minister to me, I turned the other cheek. I knew the right answers to my faith problem, but I didn't want to hear them again, didn't want to admit the reason God wasn't answering my prayers had more to do with His desire to change my heart than it did not changing my sons' heart.

The Right Things Don't Work?

I've spent the last seven years working hard to be the best mom I can be. My husband and I are doing everything we think is right for our kids . . . trying so hard to give them the best chance at choosing God . . . following heart-first (and head-first) after what we believe God has called us to as a family.

And you know what? It isn't working.

My boys drive me to the brink of insanity at least once a day. Sometimes they hate school. Some days they hate me. My husband and I bicker and fight over stupid stuff at least once a month. Some months we struggle financially. Others we struggle to keep the house clean. At least five mornings a week I wake up with a messy kitchen because I was just too tired to clean it up the night before. My bedroom is usually a mess, even though I long for it to be a haven for my husband and me. My boys fight and act out, and recently, my oldest pointed a gun at my face when I told him no.

It wasn't a real gun . . .

But it made me crumble into a pile of snotty mess crying out to the Lord, "Why God? Why do I deserve this? I TRY SO HARD to do things the right way. I've given up so much, done everything I can possibly do to give them what they need. I've loved them so hard, prayed so well, tried so hard . . . "

If I'm honest, I'm hurt Lord . . . surprised by your lack of response in my time of need. Don't you know I write about prayer? Write about raising kids? How can I write about prayer when You don't even answer mine??

Ugly, I know.

In the midst of that ugly place, I felt God calling me to get up and follow Him one more time . . . but I wan't sure that I could. It reminds me a bit of Peter and the disciples . . .

Casting Your Net

"On one occasion, while the crowd was pressing in on him to hear the word of God, he was standing by the lake of Gennesaret, and he saw two boats by the lake, but the fishermen had gone out of them and were washing their nets. Getting into one of the boats, which was Simon's, he asked him to put out a little from the land. And he sat down and taught the people from the boat. And when he had finished speaking, he said to Simon, 'Put out into the deep and let down your nets for a catch.' And Simon answered, 'Master, we toiled all night and took nothing! But at your word I will let down the nets.' And when they had done this, they enclosed a large number of fish, and their nets were breaking. They signaled to their partners in the other boat to come and help them. And they came and filled both the boats, so that they began to sink. But when Simon Peter saw it, he fell down at Jesus' knees, saying, 'Depart from me, for I am a sinful man, O Lord.' For he and all who were with him were astonished at the catch of fish that they had taken." (Luke 5:1-9)

Peter had worked hard all night long at his job, trying to catch fish, and hadn't caught even one. He'd sweat over dirty, hard, long hours of labor, to no avail.

In those days, I imagine an empty net meant an empty stomach, empty table, empty mouths, and maybe, for Peter, an empty heart. I can almost hear him thinking, "All that work for NOTHING! Wasted effort, wasted time. I should just quit." Ever felt that way, mom? Useless? Overlooked? A failure? Me too.

Sometime after this wasted fishing night, the Savior of the world, Jesus, found Himself in need of a platform . . . a safe place to stand and be sheltered so He could share His message of hope and healing. The crowds, desperate for a word drop of water when the voice of God had been silent in their land for four hundred years, were pressing in all around Him. He looked around and found a simple fisherman, with a simple fishing boat, and a simple fishing life, who was simply weary, and asked for shelter. He taught the soul-hungry people for a time, and then told the weary man Simon Peter to cast his net in the deep one more time.

Can you imagine Peter's response? Can you picture him, head in hands, eyes tired from lack of sleep, and heart weary from the weight of failure, answering the man Jesus?

"Lord, we have been out here all night. We've worked our fingers to the bone trying to provide for our families, trying to take care of them and give them our best. We've given our all, all night long and it hasn't been enough. We're tired. And we don't want to try again. Not even one more time. But because you seem to be something special, we will. Just this once, and don't ask us to do it again if you please."

You know what happened.

Peter's choice to blow on the flame of hope one last time nearly sank his boat with success. He knew at once that he had been in the presence of greatness, and knowing it, repented, left his nets, and followed Jesus.

Friends, I can't promise your next act of obedience will produce the fruit in your children's hearts you've been craving. I can't promise you that following Christ, even just one more time, will bring immediate change or smashing success.

The number one question I get asked as someone who writes about raising boys is this: how can I raise my sons to love the Lord?

My answer? You can't.

Because salvation doesn't come by the work of our hands.

There's nothing we can do to earn our own salvation, and there's nothing we can do to earn our children's salvation. No amount of good parenting, wise decisions, prayer, sacrifice, or challenges overcome will bring salvation to our homes. Because salvation is not built on works. Not even good works. Not even awesome works.

We are mistaken if we believe our good parenting moves God in any way to act on our behalf. And while it's not wrong of us to long for the salvation of our homes, it IS wrong for us to believe God brings salvation in response to our behavior.

Everything God does, He does for Himself.

"Thus says the Lord God: 'It is not for your sake, O house of Israel, that I am about to act, but for the sake of My holy Name.'" (Ezekiel 36:22)

We are part of HIS story, not the other way around. And I don't know why. I don't know why my pain or yours sometimes brings God more glory than our happiness. I don't understand why God doesn't answer my desperate prayers in a way that eases my suffering in this life. But God is not bound to give me abundance by some code of excellence on my part. And what works for your family may not come close to working for mine. Because God created our hearts and He knows the best way to reach them.

Doesn't seem fair does it?

But what is fairness in the eyes of God? Are the circumstances of my life really not fair? Do I really not get what I deserve when I work so hard? That's probably what Peter thought as he drew the net in empty for the last time. But may I submit a different notion?

My life, your life, is NOT fair in any way. It's really not fair that I have two healthy children. It's not fair that I wake up warm each morning and have plenty to eat. It's not fair that my car works and my home keeps me safe. It's not fair that I have access to the medicines I need, or that I can vote and worship freely with no threat of persecution. I don't deserve a decent paycheck or socks without holes. I don't deserve the love of a husband or new clothes.

Want fair? Want what we deserve? Fair is eternal punishment for our sins. Hell is what we deserve.

But He gave us Jesus.

The kindness of God in giving me His son led me to repentance . . . salvation. I wasn't won to Christ by promises of what He could do on my behalf. I didn't choose to believe because He promised me wealth, success, or the salvation of my children. I followed Him because I was a sinner in need of grace. I followed Him because I was found guilty in a court of heavenly law. And when my sins were called in, He stepped in to take my punishment.

So yeah . . . sometimes I feel hopeless. Sometimes I get angry at God when He doesn't do what I know He can do on my behalf. I get tired of casting the same net over and over again and coming up empty.

And then I remember the magnitude of what He has already done for me. I remember all things ultimately bring Him glory, and whatever He does do on my behalf is to make Himself known in all the land.

I don't have to understand it. I just have to look to the Cross to believe it.

No, I can't promise your obedience will bring about the change you long to see in the hearts of your children. But I can promise that holding out that flicker of hope, just enough to propel your feet forward in one more step of faith, matters to God. He sees you, and He knows what it will require to pursue your heart. He'll pursue it with reckless abandon, just because He loves you that much. But in the same way that He loves you, the same way He'll move all of heaven to chase your heart and make it His, He also loves your children. When they break your heart, they break His. When they run away from you, they run away from Him. When they reject your love, they reject His. When they refuse to walk in obedience to you, they refuse to walk in obedience to Him. He hurts with you.

But His plans for you, and your children, are good.

Choose this day . . .

Will you make a commitment with me today friends? Can we stand together, unified by Christ and our love for our children, and covenant with the Lord that we will never, ever give up on our children? And can we likewise covenant with the Lord that we will never give up on His ability to move in the hearts of our children, in spite of us?

If so, proudly proclaim your commitment by sharing it with at least one other person today and asking him/her to hold you accountable. Maybe even share your decision to never give up on Facebook, Twitter, or wherever your friends and their friends come together. Let's pray that our commitments catch on and spread like wildfire.

Consider liking our Facebook page, and then sharing these words on your Facebook wall?

"I believe God's plans for me are good. Therefore, I commit today that I will never give up on my family, and I will never give up on God's ability to move in their hearts. With His help, I will take the next step of faith even when I feel I can't, because He is the God of miracles. If you're ready to make this commitment too, copy and paste this on your wall. @Hope for the Weary Mom"

(where @Hope for the Weary Mom is an in-comment link)

Or these on Twitter?

"I will never give up on my family, & I will never give up on God's ability to move in their hearts. #WearyMom"

I believe God will meet us and fill our nets as we trust Him enough to cast just one more time.

Get in the boat with me?

Chapter Eight Study Questions

1. Have you ever felt like Peter did after that night of fishing? Ever wondered how in the world you would ever find the strength to try one more time?

2. Describe a time when you wanted to give up.

3. What does "God meeting you in your mess" mean to you? Do you expect God to change your environment, or to get it in with you, giving you the tools you need to make it?

4. Are you ready to proclaim to the world that you will never give up on your family and never give up on God's ability to work in the hearts of your children?

5. Toward the end of this book, you'll find a Weary Mom Manifesto you can print and hang in your home to remind you never to give up on your family. Print it out now.

9

When the World Presses In

Most of the stories you've heard so far in this book fall into the category of the everyday weariness all moms experience from time-to-time. But there are moms who experience a weariness that goes far beyond the ordinary. As we planned for this book, Stacey and I felt it was so very important to find a way to bring hope to that mom too. So we prayed and asked God if there was someone we could ask to share her personal testimony of God's grace in a mess that goes much deeper than what either of us has ever experienced.

After turning down an interview with Oprah Winfrey, my friend Tracey graciously allowed me the honor of talking to her about "the mess" of losing her only son. Her prayer is that her story might bring you comfort and help you place your hope in the God who met her there.

Her story, and mine, starts in a small town...

***

Narrows is a sleepy little town in southwestern Virginia. Known for its love of football and people, Narrows is home to a long stretch of the New River—the world's third oldest river geologically speaking (according to Wikipedia) and one of only a few rivers in the world that flows north instead of south. There is one stoplight regulating traffic out of Narrows, one fast food restaurant, one amazing mom and pop restaurant called Anna's, one grade school, one middle school, and one high school. We are the mighty Greenwave, and please don't put an "s" on the end to make us plural. We are one.

In a small town, everyone knows everyone else. Sometimes this is a good thing, and sometimes it's not, but most of the time, the feeling of knowing and being known helps you bypass any hard feelings about it. If you make a mistake in Narrows, most of the community knows about it in time to discuss it over breakfast the next morning. They'll have opinions about what you did and say things like, "her poor mama," or "bless her heart," but they'll also be the first ones to put their arms around you when you go to the altar to repent on Sunday morning.

The churches in Narrows are like extended family. There's one Baptist church, one Methodist, one Christian, and a few others located throughout town, but by and large the community lives out life together. Your friends across the river won't end up in a different school district than you, and you certainly won't have to play against them in football. My dad probably played ball with yours in school, and my mama hosted the Circle meetings of First Baptist for yours once a year.

Overall, it's a peaceful, beautiful little town. Nothing ever happens much in or to the people of Narrows.

Until one day it did.

It was a blustery Monday morning on April 16, 2007. Snow flurries found their way to southwestern Virginia on a day that should have been filled with spring warmth. Students wrapped up in coats crossed the Drillfield at Virginia Tech, pulled into parking spaces, said goodbye to friends, and sat down in their desks to learn . . . just like any other day.

Tracey Lane, a long time resident of Narrows, got up, fixed breakfast, and went to work in nearby Pulaski, VA. She still felt the high of the beautiful weekend she'd just had with her family. They'd gotten the great news that her son, Jarrett, had gotten a teaching assistant scholarship at Florida State University in the engineering department, and that news significantly eased the financial burden of Jarrett's education, something she'd been worrying about for some time.

The day before, Jarrett responded to an altar call at First Baptist Church, and proudly told the congregation about the way God had provided for him, publicly thanking God for taking such good care of His children.

Tracey was so proud of all he'd become.

She thought back to what they had survived as a family . . . the divorce of her parents, her own divorce, the death of her older brother and two step siblings . . . and felt like maybe they were finally hitting their stride. She said a silent "thank You, God," and then went to work.

Sometime that morning, Tracey heard the news of a shooting at Virginia Tech, where Jarrett was attending college. Some friends encouraged her to call and check on

Jarrett, and she did, but felt sure he was safe even when she couldn't reach him. She thought to herself, "Surely he went back to his apartment after the shooting and is waiting it out like everyone else."

She left him a message and went back to work.

A few hours later, after hours of not being able to reach him, Tracey began to worry. The only man in the family, it was unlike Jarrett to leave his mom and two sisters hanging. She knew him well enough to know that if he were safe, he would want her to know. Visions of him being in the hospital, helping the wounded, or in a room somewhere with survivors began to fill her head, and she told her boss she was going home. She prayed for his safety the whole way.

After her daughters tried with no luck to locate Jarrett in one of the three surrounding hospitals, and they hadn't heard from him all day, Tracey knew of only one thing she could do. She grabbed her purse, opened her front door, and ran smack into her family's deacon at First Baptist Church. She looked at him and said, "I'm going to find my baby." His reply? "I'm taking you."

***

I picked up my two-year-old from the sitter and planted myself in front of the TV after work, much like every other person in the world that day. My cell phone rang again and I picked it up quickly thinking it was my husband, who had been on campus all day as a part of the emergency response team. It wasn't. It was his brother. "Have you heard from

Cory? Can you reach him? Does he know who's dead? Tracey Lane hasn't been able to reach Jarrett all day and he had class in that building this morning. Is there anything Cory can do to find out?"

I promised to do my best to contact my husband and hit the end button on my phone. But before I could even dial his number, my cell phone rang again . . .

"Tracey just got word. Jarrett is dead."

***

Just after 7:15 on the morning of April 16, 2007, two students were shot to death inside of West Ambler Johnson Hall. Approximately two hours later, and all the way across campus, Seung-Hui Cho barricaded the doors of Norris Hall and began a killing spree that would take the lives of 32 people and wound 17 others. Screams pierced the silence. Students began jumping out of windows, hiding in bathrooms, diving under tables, and under the bodies of their murdered friends for shelter. One girl, so traumatized by what she had seen, jumped out the window of her classroom and sprinted all the way across campus before collapsing in front of the basketball coliseum. Mass chaos ensued and ended only with the gunman's suicide as he heard the police ramming down the doors.

Jarrett Lane, a promising student, vibrant young man, member of the church I grew up in, and precious son of Tracey Lane, lost his life in the Virginia Tech massacre. His death rocked the sleepy town of Narrows, VA, and plunged a community, a nation, into mourning.

As I write this chapter, it's been five years since Jarrett's death. Tracey no longer gets phone calls or flowers on a daily basis, and since that time, she's gone back to school, given back to her community and church, and tried to help her family and community heal. She's living proof that there's hope after significant and traumatic loss, and is eager to tell the world about God's grace as she walked through this mess. What follows are four ways Tracey believes God provided for her before and during her walk through grief. Consider them her words of wisdom, just for you.

1. Build your foundation now.

As I spoke with Tracey for this chapter, the passage from Luke 6:47-48 came to mind:

"Everyone who comes to me and hears my words and does them, I will show you what he is like: he is like a man building a house, who dug deep and laid the foundation on the rock. And when a flood arose, the stream broke against that house and could not shake it, because it had been well built."

I think it's important to start with the fact Tracey had built "her house," or life, on the rock before tragedy took her son from her. A life spent serving the church, time in the Word, consistent growth in her walk with Christ—these were the things that made her foundation secure, so that when the rains came, she was able to come out on the other side of the storm standing.

Her house was well-built.

What does that mean? It means that a long time before Jarrett died, Tracey had given her life to Jesus and was pursuing an intimate relationship with Him. She had already settled the answers to many of the questions that would assail her during that time of grief, and was able to cling to the truth of God's Word because she had already seen Him prove Himself to her over and over again.

My guess is that Tracey never thought her years spent pursuing a deep relationship with Christ would be needed to prepare her for losing her son in such a horrific way. But then, isn't that just the point? None of us knows what the day will bring, or when the storms will come. We look at our children and dream about what they'll become, but do we entertain the notion that they might not grow up? Might not become who we thought God had made them to be? No, at least not for any length of time. It's just too painful to think about our children dying before us. Rightfully so.

And while it isn't a popular thing to say, many of the students and teachers who died that day did so without Christ. Entire families were left to grieve alone, without the hope of heaven. And in Tracey's words, "I can't even imagine not having God to carry me through this."

The point? Build your house on the rock of God's Word, the truth of who His Son is and what He did now. Don't wait until tomorrow to get to know the God who loved you enough to send His only Son to die for your sins. And don't be content with just believing the basic tenants of the Christian faith. Build.

Build.

Step One: If you haven't placed your faith in Jesus as your Savior, do it now. If you need help knowing how to do that, email Stacey and me privately at hopeforthewearymom@gmail.com.

Step Two: Find a group of local believers (Christians who meet together on a regular basis) and start going. They won't be perfect, but commit to learning more about what it means to walk out the Christian faith with them by your side.

Step Three: Find time every day to pray and get to know God through His Word. Ask God to make the Bible come alive to you, speak to your life situation, and provide the guidance you need to follow after Him.

Step Four: Say "yes" to God. Commit to obeying His Word and ask Him to give you the strength you need to do it.

These steps aren't foolproof, and they don't guarantee protection from the "nonsensicals" of life. Bad things will still happen to you after you become a Christian. In fact, really bad things might happen to you. But you will be prepared because you've built, laid a firm foundation on one, unchanging piece of Truth.

God's love.

2. Try hard not to walk through life alone.

The reason I described the little town of Narrows in such detail at the beginning of this chapter is because it was the very nature of a small town that played a huge part in Tracey's healing.

Within minutes of hearing about the shootings, and piecing together the idea that Tracey's son might not be coming home, Tracey's deacon just showed up on her doorstep. My heart just bursts with pride at the way he and the people of Narrows swooped in and cared for Tracey and her family in real, tangible ways after Jarrett's death.

Everyone wanted to help. Everyone grieved. And in ways as simple as freezable food, beautiful flowers, and even holding her as she found out the news that would change her life, the people of Narrows and its surrounding towns reached out to let her know she wasn't alone.

Many of the students killed that day were from big cities, where neighbors don't know each other as well, and church members may not even know each other's names. Parents and siblings were left to deal with their losses alone, unrecognized by their communities and peers. And that just seems so very sad.

Now I realize that not everyone can live in a small town. My husband and I left Narrows over 10 years ago ourselves. It's not possible for everyone to have an entire community surround them during tragedy. But it is possible to invest in a sample of your community, regardless of its size.

Are you invested in a church? Have you joined a Sunday school class, or small group? Are you investing in the lives of others, living out your life alongside of other people, sharing your journey? If not, start making steps in that direction today. My husband's work schedule makes it very easy for us to be isolated. It requires a substantial amount of effort to make ourselves get up on Sunday morning when he's worked until 3:00am the night before. It isn't easy for him to stay out late for group activities or time with friends on a Friday night when he has to be up at 5:00am the next morning. But we do it.

Why?

Because we are from a small town. And we believe God designed Christians to love, support, and live out life with other Christians.

The fact of the matter is, it doesn't matter if you live in a small town or not. If you choose not to invest in relationships, they won't be there when you need them most. Make a choice today to open your life and heart, and pray that God will bring you friends to do life with.

3. Keep talking to God.

In our interview, I asked Tracey if she ever experienced any anger with God over Jarrett's death. Her reply? "Of course. But He's big enough to handle anything I throw His way."

"When I asked God why He took my son—so full of life, such a bright future—when I was tempted to get mad at God, or walk away from Him, I remembered all the days of our lives are written in His book. Not one of us is promised tomorrow. I believe Jarrett's time on this earth was done. He had fulfilled his mission, left his legacy, and I have peace knowing I was the best mother for him I possibly could have been. That helps me have peace. The gunman at Virginia Tech did not take my son's life. God's plan for him had simply been fulfilled."

God already knows what's in your heart friends. He knows if you're mad at Him, feeling distant, or distrusting of His motives and love. Remember this: Christ died while we were yet sinners (Romans 5:8). That means Jesus willingly endured the shame and brutality of a death on the cross knowing you and I were going to sin. In fact, while we were still sinning, entrenched in only caring about our own selfish gain, laughing at His ways and His love, He pursued us with all the power of heaven. Why? Because of His great love. It's a love like no other. And it's big enough to handle all your emotions, and mine.

Tell Him how you feel. Confess your emotions, doubts, and deep concerns to Him, and allow Him to prove His love to you all over again. Just run to His arms. They're big enough to hold you.

4. Refuse to let go of hope.

If there's one thing Tracey really wants other moms who have experienced tragedies, losses, or loss of dreams for their children to know, it's this:

"There is life beyond the tragedy. It's hard to see that or accept it when you're right in the middle. There will be days that the pain of your loss will threaten to overcome you, take you away to a place you don't want to go. But one day, you'll wake up and notice the sky is a beautiful shade of blue. You'll see the glory of the clouds and remember how much you loved them. You'll feel the warmth of the sun, laugh at a joke, smile at a stranger, and remember life can be good. When that day comes, hold it in your heart, because you've been given a gift from God. Pass it on. Comfort others with the comfort you've been given and watch what joy that brings to your life."

After my miscarriage, and the five other significant losses I suffered leading up to it, I closed the lid on my prayer life for several months. Slowly, but surely, I've been reopening that lid. But there are still pieces of my heart that are learning how to trust God after so much hurt. I think He's ok with that.

I've learned it's foolish to rush grief, and that grief winds its way through our hearts and minds, affecting layers we didn't know we even had.

Sometimes we just have to give ourselves time and admit we're helpless to change by ourselves.

Mark Batterson, in his best-selling book, *The Circle Maker*, says, "...raw dependence is the raw material out of which God performs His greatest miracles."

I'm pretty sure God allows suffering and challenge in our lives to bring us to a place of raw dependence.

I'm NOT saying my child, or Tracey's, died just so we could be more like Jesus. But I AM saying it would be a waste not to let them make us more like Jesus . . .

My time with Tracey was such a gift, and I'm so grateful to her for allowing me into this sacred part of her heart. One of the things she said that I don't think I'll ever forget was that she knew Jarrett wouldn't want her life to stop because of his death. She knew from the beginning that this would be the hardest season she would ever walk through, but knowing how much Jarrett loved life, how much he wanted to give and get everything he could from life while he was here, helped her to want to love life again too.

Every day, every breath we're given is a gift from God.

Grab on to hope and don't let go.

Chapter Nine Study Questions

1. In this chapter, Brooke acknowledges there are moms whose weariness goes beyond the normal day-to-day most of us experience, and uses the story of a mom who lost her child in a traumatic way to illustrate her points. But it's important to note that trauma isn't only defined by death. Maybe you've had to say good-bye to a dream. Maybe your precious child was born with limitations that make life more challenging for you than others. Or maybe you're raising your children alone. All of these situations fall within the realm of the weariness described in this chapter.

2. One of the most important things that helped Tracey as she struggled to stand through the loss of her son was a pre-laid foundation of truth and love in Christ. What's one thing you can do starting today to continue the building process of your faith?

3. Not everyone has the ability or even desire to live in a small town, but we can all have a piece of the "small-town mentality" in the way we open ourselves to relationships. How are you investing in the people God has brought into your life? What's one thing you can begin to do differently that will strengthen your relationships?

4. When we're in the midst of significant trauma, it can be tempting to quit talking to God because we don't trust Him as much as we used to. Have you ever walked through a season like this? If so, describe what it felt like.

5. Is it hard or easy for you to see that there's life after loss? Do you find that Tracey's encouragement and personal testimony give you hope for that day to come?

10

When Weary Moms Walk Together

I watch them arrive in groups of two-three with diapers bags and kids in tow. A few moms walk in alone and anxiously scout out a place to sit at one of the seven tables that fill the room. Each of the seven tables is decorated with flowers and chocolate in the most thoughtful way. Scattered around the room are several women waiting with open hearts and arms ready to hug. Mamas let out heavy sighs of release as kids are safely tucked in the age appropriate classes. Food is served buffet style alongside a steamy hot cup of coffee. Everyone settles in their seats ready for the first Kitchen Table Talk to begin in Austin, Texas. All eyes look to Brooke and then to me and I whisper a prayer:

"Lord, only you can fill their hearts. Speak through us. Use our stories and words. Bring hope to these women today."

As we begin to share, the women ease a bit into their seats. Some take notes. Others dot their eyes with the tissues sweetly provided on the tables. God honors His Word once again, "For where two or three are gathered in my name, there am I among them," (Matthew 18:20). He comes to us like rain and waters the dry places. He moves in and through our hearts and does exactly what He promised He would. His very presence reminds us we are not alone, and the filled-up tables testify that we have sisters who we can walk with in the weary days motherhood sometimes brings.

***

The truth is, what we really need is Jesus. But He knows, more than we do, that we were made to live in community. He has always been a fan of the buddy system. After all, didn't Adam have Eve? Naomi had Ruth, and Abraham was promised generations as numerous as the stars in the sky. He never planned on us living a hope filled life alone. His design was that we would walk with others for a lifetime.

But sometimes, life gets busy with diapers and chores and getting through the day and we forget what we were made for. We forget our design. We don't even realize we miss it until one day we are alone and desperate for just one person to know our hearts. At other times, we are called to a foreign land and we are alone don't know a soul there. What do we do on those days?

A few years ago, I found myself in exactly that same situation. I have always been a girl who loves connecting with other women. I have joined Bible studies and led small groups numerous times. My heart loves nothing more than meeting friends for coffee and catching a chick flick. But suddenly I was in a new town, with a three year old and a baby. My husband had a new job working long hours and I was alone much of the day. I remember after my daughter was born, shortly before Christmas, the nurse said to me, "Isn't anyone going to come and see you?" Hormonal obviously, I held back tears and said, "We just moved here. I don't know anyone." I think that made her feel worse than I did at the time. She made a point to come visit me while I was recovering.

After bringing home my bundle of Christmas Grace, no one brought food. We had no visitors. We eagerly awaited the arrival of family who would come after the holidays to help us settle in our new home and with our newest addition. Their visit seemed all too short and once again I faced long days and nights feeling disconnected.

I did what I knew to do. I cried out to the Lord. I had a really long talk with Him one evening on my way to the grocery store. I told Him I was tired and lonely. What I really needed, I reminded Him, was someone to say my name.

Does that sound silly to you? Well, remember, I grew up in a small town. The old saying "Everybody knows everybody" is true. I went to college where I had a few good friends already. I roomed with lifelong friends who knew me. This was the first time in my life I did not really know anyone. And no one, I mean no one, knew my name. So this mattered a great deal to me.

I grabbed my cart and tried to remember what we needed in our pantry at home. I was every kind of weary and worn. I looked it, too. My hair was a mess and I'm not sure I had bothered doing my make up that day. I noticed the two girls almost immediately when I started down the aisle. They were having way too much fun for me. Clearly, they were friends enjoying an inside joke. I found myself annoyed and jealous at the same time. I passed by them quickly reaching for a jar of canned spaghetti sauce. When I got to the end of the aisle, one of the girls said, "She wants to know if your name is Stacey." I stopped suddenly in my tracks. "Did she just say my name? MY NAME?" I looked back at the girls searching their faces for familiarity. "Yes," I said, "that is my NAME."

As it turns out, the girl who knew me was an old friend from college. I did not recognize her because she had dyed her hair blonde. She was living and working in town for a short time. We chatted and exchanged numbers. She left and I went back to shopping. As I made my way to the parking lot I was overcome with tears once again. "Lord, you can do anything. You really do know my heart. And you have not for one minute lost sight of me. Thank you."

Over the next couple of years, God began to build community in my life. I found a sweet group of sisters to share life with on a daily basis. We gathered around a table and studied God's Word and our hearts connected deeply. They showed up in droves when our third daughter arrived with enough food to feed an army. It may have been because I told them this story and they felt sad for little, lonely me a few years before. The contrast was amazing. I smiled at the way God had provided. I also enjoyed being spoiled.

Still, I will not discount the lonely years. They served a purpose in my life. I walked closely with Jesus because I did not have anyone else other than my husband and my girls to cling to. I look at those days as a time where He was doing a specific work. I am grateful now for those days. But, I can also see how He was working behind the scenes and preparing me for a new, richer community of women who became sisters of my heart.

Where are you today friend? Are you weary and alone? Do you desire a rich community of women to walk through the mothering years beside you? Do you know there is one simple thing you can do right now to begin to see this happen in your life?

Ask God to bring a friend into your life.

We don't know how or when God will bring this about for you. But we believe God with you, that He will begin to build a community of other moms in your life. Why? We have seen Him do that in our own lives. We've lived weary and alone, and we've seen the fruit that comes from trusting God and sharing our lives with others who understand. Here are few things you need to keep in mind:

- God has a plan, and He sometimes does not work on our timetable. Building deep community takes time. But the good news is you can start now.
- You may have to be brave and step out of your comfort zone. When we moved to our new town, I had to put on my brave shoes many times and initiate conversations with strangers. Some of those friendships did not last. Some stuck and are still with me today.
- Building community always brings a risk factor, because other people are human just like we are. We need grace from them just like they need it from us. We didn't say community was perfect.
- While you are waiting, continue let God mold and make you into the woman He wants you to be. Don't wait.

Walk with Him now. It is true, you have to be the friend others want to have in order to get a friend you want to keep.

- Friends don't complete us. Friends compliment us. Only God can fill your heart with hope. True friends will point you to Him.

In the Mean Time

Sometimes it takes a while for the truth to sink in. When we're weary, hurt, and disappointed with life it can be good to open our hearts to others and walk through the valley willingly together. We know it can be scary to think of opening up those dark places to others, but there's really nothing to be afraid of when you embrace the truths we've set before you in *Hope for the Weary Mom*:

- We've been loved into repentance by Jesus. He loved us while we were drowning in our sin. He sees us, loves us, and promises to redeem our hurts if we'll open ourselves to Him.
- We don't have to measure up. There is no perfect mom out there, and if there's one who says she is, she's lying. When you look at other moms, other women, choose to believe they're more like you than they are different. Refuse to allow the voice of the enemy (who only wants to kill, steal, and destroy you) to be the loudest voice you hear. Fill your head and heart with the Word. Let God's voice be the one you nurture.
- Acknowledge you're really not enough for the job. You don't have what it takes to be the kind of mom you want to be and you can't change your children's hearts no matter how much you try. Parenting is not a solo act. Just

as it takes the Creator God to breath life into our wombs, it takes the Redeemer God to turn hearts of stone to hearts of flesh (Ezekiel 36:26).

- Set aside regular times to renew your strength from the Lord. Meditate on His Word and allow the truth of it to change the way you act, the way you believe. Choose to believe that it's true and walk out obedience to it every day. If you need practical help doing that, visit Stacey's blog, or Brooke's blog. We both talk regularly about living out faith.
- Make a commitment today to try one more time. The times when you're the weariest are the times when it's most important to remember your commitment to never give up believing in God's ability to move in the hearts of your family.
- Go to God when you've messed up. Make an altar to Him wherever you are and confess your sins, expecting Him to lovingly pick you up and dust you off.
- Choose to love Him and follow Him no matter what. Expect hard times, and choose this day who you will serve. When things don't go the way you want them to, cling all the more tightly to the God who never changes, the same one who gave up His Son so you could find forgiveness from sin.

May we encourage you to gather together with a group of your friends, online or off, to get real and share the cobwebs of your soul? Jesus promises to meet you there. And not only will He meet you in your mess friend, He'll hold your hand and walk you through it.

***

The neatest thing happened in Austin toward the end of our first Kitchen Table Talk. We gave the women time to share their hearts and talk through some discussion questions at their tables. What began as a hushed chat turned into a lively discussion among friends. They talked long. They laughed together and bonded over the similarities of their stories. Hearts connected. In fact, we had to interrupt them to conclude or time together. The only complaint we had about our time together was it was too short.

Weary moms joined hands and began to walk together. It was a beautiful thing.

Chapter Ten Study Questions

1. Who are you walking with through the motherhood years? Can you call her (or them) at any time of day and ask for prayer or encouragement?

2. Have you ever had a particularly lonely season in your life? How did God provide for your heart during that time?

3. Tell about a time when you were brave and sought out a new friend.

4. What are you doing to cultivate your friendship with Jesus?

5. How can you connect with other weary moms and walk together?

Questions and Answers

with Stacey Thacker and Brooke McGlothlin

We asked you to share some of the burning questions on your mind about the authors behind *Hope for the Weary Mom*. Nothing was off limits! We picked our favorites and are thrilled to be sharing a little bit of our behind the scenes with you, friends! Here we go!

1. How did you come to Christ?

Stacey

I don't remember not going to church. As a child I grew up knowing that "Jesus loved me. . . for the Bible tells me so." This is mostly because my mom rededicated her life to Christ right before I was born. She was faithful to not only take me to church but also demonstrate to me a life of faith built on prayer and the study of God's Word. I accepted Christ at age nine when I read a book my pastor gave me on how to become a Christian. Shortly after that, I was baptized.

It wasn't until I was a student at Indiana University that my rooted faith began to grow. I became involved with a Christian student group called Campus Crusade for Christ and learned what it meant to walk with Christ in the daily aspects of life, share His love with others, and study God's Word with focused determination. I went on mission trips, led small groups, and found a passion to serve God with my whole life.

Brooke

I was raised in a sweet little Southern Baptist church in southwestern Virginia. My Sundays were filled with sound biblical teaching, and adults who loved me. I was saved and baptized when I was just nine years old, but didn't really start walking closely with the Lord until right before my husband and I started dating in 1999. Ironically, just before we got together, my husband and I had both decided that doing things our way wasn't working, and entered our relationship committed to doing things God's way from the very beginning.

2. How did you meet your husband?

Stacey

My husband Mike and I met on a Campus Crusade for Christ Mission Project in Ocean City, New Jersey the summer of 1991. He was a student at Miami of Ohio and I was attending Indiana University. We both knew from the beginning that this was "the one." We dated long distance for two years before email and cell phones existed. He was a true gentleman, and paid for my phone bills! We married in April 1994.

Brooke

I've had a crush on my husband since the third grade. Corny, I know, but it's true. When I was an awkward little girl in grade school this family of all boys moved to our small town and started attending our church. The three brothers, all pretty handsome, were all the rage for quite some time, but my heart belonged to the youngest.

Like all the other girls, I giggled when he walked by, asked him if he would be my boyfriend (he said no), and bought a copy of the school picture he was selling. For just 50 cents I had a picture of the guy for me, nerdy glasses and all.

In the eighth grade, I asked him to go to a dance with me. Well, to be more correct, I had my best friend Jennifer call him and ask if he would go with me to the dance. He said no (again!).

After several hits, misses, and almosts throughout the years, his family began scheming to get us together. I was spending a good deal of time walking with his sister-n-law, Susan, and often, after a hard walk, she would invite me in for lemonade, a movie, or just to chat. Miraculously, he would show up needing to use their weight room, or talk to his big brother about something, or just work on his truck. We started spending a lot of time together because of our mutual relationships with his brother and sister-n-law, but I was dating someone else, and wasn't sure I wanted to throw that relationship away.

One day, after yet another walk with Susan, he offered to drive me home. Now my parents lived just up the street, and he and I both knew I didn't really need to be driven home. I tried to tell him no (honestly, I did!) but he was insistent, so I climbed up in the truck, watched his brother and sister-n-law wave at us, and let him drive me home.

When we got there (30 seconds later) he turned the truck off, looked into my eyes, and told me I was the girl for him . . . the one he'd been looking for all of his life, but didn't know was right in front of him. He respectfully acknowledged I was dating someone else, but asked for a chance to prove himself to me.

We started dating about two months later . . . and he's been the love of my life ever since.

3. What's the biggest bit of parenting advice you wholeheartedly believe in but have trouble practicing?

Stacey

This is such a great question. The one that comes to mind currently is "Life is not an emergency," By Ann Voskamp. I'm not sure it is really parenting advice but in my home this is a real issue. As you know, we have four girls. Everything in my home seems to be an emergency. Lost shoes? Emergency! Where is the remote? Emergency! She is looking cross eyed at me? Emergency! I try very hard to live above the drama, but I am not always successful. I'm praying God will help me stay calm and not contribute to the emotion. The trouble is, as a one-of-a-kind family, we tend to feed off each other. I know getting enough rest and finding times to just be quiet during my day helps me maintain calm. I am taking baby steps in this area. I wonder if other girl households can relate!

Brooke

Don't yell at your kids. Ouch! It hurts to admit that, but it's true. I try SO hard not to yell at my boys, but sometimes I feel like if I don't yell, they'll never hear me over all of the boy noise. Our home is loud most of the time, and our youngest son is just naturally a loud kid. I often find myself raising my voice just to be heard! I lose my cool with them a lot more than I care to admit, but I am getting better at it every day, and I try hard to tell them (and show them) I love them twice as much as I lose it with them.

4. As weary moms (and women in general), how do we encourage each other to quit pretending that everything is OK, and just get real with each other?

Stacey

I think we have to be willing to tell our own stories. I love that this book is giving some weary moms permission to do so. There is true power in sharing our hearts with other women. Because when we do that, we have the chance to connect on a real level. We can spur one another on and we can pray for each other. As I look back on this past year and the journey with *Hope* I am amazed at how many moms thought they were alone. I love we all know, now, that we are not.

The truth is, the parts of our stories that are not so bright and shiny are what people most want to hear about. It helps them know they are normal. I think we hide because the enemy has convinced us no one will understand and everyone will think we are crazy. This simply is not the case. We need to tell what is really going on. We can share our story and in the process pass hope on to another mom.

Brooke

I love this question!

I come from a very private family who likes to keep their "business" (you really have to say that with a southern accent to get the full effect) to themselves. I get asked a lot about why I share my junk openly, and my answer is always the same:

a. I want to know if I'm normal or not.
b. So that in the rare event that I actually do something right, another mom might benefit.

Seriously though, I think we all need to quit pretending that the last 50 years of women's lib haven't affected how we think about ourselves. I'm grateful for the opportunity to vote, and share my opinions as much as the next woman, but in spite of everything freedom for women got right, I think we also got some things wrong. After years of being told that we can have it all, we feel guilty, or like there's something wrong with us, if we're not doing a good job of it. So we don't talk about it. I've found that by laying my mess out for all the world to see, other women have been freed up to do the same. And the effects are far-reaching! When we admit our weaknesses, we give God permission to be strong for us (but I've already written about that)!

The best way you can encourage other moms to get real about their messes is by getting real about yours. Gently and humbly come alongside one or two moms to start with, and watch what God does as you let it all out.

5. How do you manage your family and your writing schedule?

Stacey

We are a busy family of six and managing life at times seems to be a farfetched dream. But there is a lot of truth in the saying that you make time for what is important. When I need to write because something is due, I write. When I need to write because I have a word I need to get out of my head and heart, I write. I can fit it in when I need to.

On a daily basis my day looks like this: I wake up at 6:15AM and have my time with Jesus. Sometimes, my response to Him is through the written word. After the girls get up, we eat, watch "I Love Lucy," and start school. I'm usually busy teaching, fixing lunch, and doing chores until early afternoon. When my toddler takes a nap, I have a little bit of time to write. She is a busy girl, and I've realized recently that writing while she is awake is hard for me.

The rest of our day is filled with ballet, daily grocery store errands, and dinner prep. By evening my brain is mush and you would not want to read what I write!

On the weekends, I try to write on Saturday morning or Sunday afternoon. My favorite place to write is at Barnes and Noble while eating a vanilla cupcake and drinking a hazelnut latte. Sadly, this happens only once in a blue moon.

Brooke

I'm not sure I'm the best person to talk about this, because I'm constantly changing how I approach it. Truthfully, in the beginning of my career I did a really poor job of it, neglecting my family so I could build what I thought was an important following. I wrote a short, inexpensive e-book about all the Lord taught me from that time called *Notes to Aspiring Writers: Your Dream, God's Plan* that really sums up my feelings about a writer's priorities. That being said, with two active young boys we homeschool, and a husband who works shift work, I have to get creative. Since they're young, I write most of the time when my boys are having quiet time or are asleep. For me that means about two hours mid-day, and another two after they've gone to bed. If I'm in a serious season of writing (such as for this book) we hire a babysitter one day a week, and I try to get up one to two hours earlier in the morning to work. It isn't perfect, but it works for us right now.

6. What are your top three reads for believing moms?

Stacey

Jesus Calling by Sarah Young – I love this devotional because it is written from the perspective of Jesus to the reader. I find this a perfect daily read when life is at its craziest. I also love the Scriptures listed at the end of each daily reading. I found out recently that this is now an app for your phone. So you can have it with you wherever you go!

Ministry of Motherhood by Sally Clarkson – This was the first book I read that helped me to see my mothering as a discipleship ministry. I realized Jesus understood my life as a mom and His training of the twelve looked a lot like my daily training and molding my girls.

Pursuit of God by A.W. Tozer – This is not a mom book exactly. But I think we need to remember who we are as women of God first. The language in this book is a bit elevated and many times I have to re-read the sentences a couple of times. But it sinks soul-deep quickly and will encourage you greatly. I went through this with a group of moms a couple years ago, and though at first they were skeptical, it became their favorite book. This book is one I have read again and again.

Brooke

One Thousand Gifts: A Dare to Live Fully Right Where You Are, by Ann Voskamp. This book is poetry, but it's so much more than that. In the day-to-day weariness of mothering, we keep the flame of hope going by choosing to be thankful for the good things in our lives. This book will teach you how to do that. It's just beautiful.

Give Them Grace: Dazzling Your Kids with the Love of Jesus, by Elyse Fitzpatrick. This book doesn't offer a cheesy "let your kids get away with everything" kind of grace. It's a deep, challenging, convicting look at how the grace of God changes everything, including how we parent our kids.

A Praying Life: Connecting with God in a Distracting World, by Paul Miller. A true, honest, and gritty look at prayer. While it's not really a parenting book, the author talks a lot about how we do our best parenting on our knees, and I wholeheartedly agree.

Help for the Weary Mom

2 Corinthians 12:9
"But he said to me, 'My grace is sufficient for you, for my power is made perfect in weaknes.' Therefore I will boast all the more gladly of my weaknesses, so that the power of Christ may rest upon me."

John 16:28
"I have said these things to you, that in me you may have peace. In the world you will have tribulation. But take heart; I have overcome the world."

Isaiah 41:10
"Fear not, for I am with you; be not dismayed, for I am your God; I will strengthen you, I will help you, I will uphold you with my righteous right hand."

Philippians 4:13
"I can do all things through Him who strengthens me."

Galatians 6:9
"And let us not grow weary of doing good, for in due season we will reap, if we do not give up."

Psalm 121: 1-4
"I lift up my eyes to the hills. From where does my help come? My help comes from the LORD, who made heaven and earth. He will not let your foot be moved; he who keeps you will not slumber. Behold, he who keeps Israel will neither slumber nor sleep."

Psalm 103: 2-5

"Bless the Lord, O my soul, and forget not all his benefits, who forgives all your iniquity, who heals all your diseases, who redeems your life from the pit, who crowns you with steadfast love and mercy, who satisfies you with good so that your youth is renewed like the eagle's."

Matthew 11:29-30

"Take my yoke upon you, and learn from me, for I am gentle and lowly in heart, and you will find rest for your souls. For my yoke is easy, and my burden is light."

Hebrews 13:20-21

"Now may the God of peace who brought again from the dead our Lord Jesus, the great shepherd of the sheep, by the blood of the eternal covenant, equip you with everything good that you may do his will, working in us that which is pleasing in his sight, through Jesus Christ, to whom be glory forever and ever. Amen."

Psalm 116:2 (NLT)

"Because he bends down to listen, I will pray as long as I have breath!"

Psalm 31:1-5

In you, O Lord, do I take refuge; let me never be put to shame; in your righteousness deliver me! Incline your ear to me; rescue me speedily! Be a rock of refuge for me, a strong fortress to save me! For you are my rock and my fortress; and for your name's sake you lead me and guide me; you take me out of the net they have hidden for me, for you are my refuge. Into your hand I commit my spirit; you have redeemed me, O Lord, faithful God."

Psalm 91:1-2

"He who dwells in the shelter of the Most High will abide in the shadow of the Almighty. I will say to the Lord, 'My refuge and my fortress, my God, in whom I trust.'"

Psalm 55:22

"Cast your burden on the LORD, and he will sustain you; he will never permit the righteous to be moved."

2 Timothy 1:7

"God gave us a spirit not of fear but of power and love and self-control."

John 14:27

"Peace I leave with you; my peace I give to you. Not as the world gives do I give to you. Let not your hearts be troubled, neither let them be afraid."

John 3:30

"He must increase, but I must decrease."

James 4:8

"Draw near to God, and he will draw near to you."

Jeremiah 29:11

"For I know the plans I have for you, declares the LORD, plans for welfare and not for evil, to give you a future and a hope."

The Weary Mom Manifesto

"I believe God's plans for me are good. Therefore, I commit today that I will never give up on my family, and I will never give up on God's ability to move in their hearts. With His help, I will take the next step of faith even when I feel I can't, because He is the God of miracles."

Name: _____

Witness: _____

Date: _____

Resources for the Weary Mom

We've put together a list of wonderful online resources just for you mamas. Take a few minutes and check them out. We pray they will bring you hope.

The MOD Squad blog (for mothers of daughters)
www.modsquadblog.com

The MOB Society blog (for mothers of boys)
www.themobsociety.com

29 Lincoln Avenue (a place to be encouraged, grow in faith, and talk about the stuff of life) www.29lincolnavenue.com

Surprised by Life (leading women in saying "yes" to God)
www.brookemcglothlin.com/blog

21 Days of Prayer for Sons www.21daysofprayerforsons.com

Parenting from the Overflow
www.parentingfromtheoverflow.com

Hope for the Weary Mom on Facebook
www.facebook.com/hopeforthewearymom

The MOD Squad on Facebook www.facebook.com/modsquad

The MOB Society on Facebook www.facebook.com/themobsociety

About the Authors

Stacey Thacker is Mike's wife and the mother of four vibrant girls. She is a believer and writer who loves God's Word and connecting with women. You can find her blogging at 29 Lincoln Avenue where she seeks to encourage your heart, grow in faith, and talk about the stuff of life. Stacey is also the co-founder of MODsquad Blog (Mother's of Daughters), Write It, Girl, and a community leader for (in)courage. Follow her on Twitter @stacey29lincoln.

Other Books by Stacey

What God Wants You to Know - a 31 Day Journey straight to the heart of the Father. He has precious truths He wants to you to know.

31 Days of Prayer for Our Daughters – with MODsquad Blog Contributors

Brooke McGlothlin is a mom of two young boys who leave her desperate for grace, knowing that if God doesn't show up, nothing happens. She's the author of the best-selling e-book *Warrior Prayers: Praying the Word for Boys In the Areas They Need It Most*, and creator of the *21 Days of Prayer for Sons* challenge. In 2010, she co-founded the well-loved online community for mothers of boys, the MOB Society.

Brooke makes her home in the mountains of Southwest Virginia with her husband—the man she's had a crush on since the 3rd grade—and spends her days writing, homeschooling their two sons, and playing with their sweet Labrador Retriever, Toby. She enjoys playing hard with her boys, searching for beauty through photography, and leading women to say "yes" to God at her personal blog, Surprised by Life. Follow her on Twitter as @BrookeWrites.

Other Books and Resources by Brooke

Warrior Prayers: Praying the Word for Boys in the Areas They Need It Most

Notes to Aspiring Writers: Your Dream, God's Plan

From Mom's Failure to God's Grace: Stories of Raising Boys from the MOB Society Writers

Surprised By Life: Five Ways to Respond Well When Life Doesn't Go as Planned

Made in the USA
Lexington, KY
14 February 2014